The "Not How I Planned It" Memoirs
BOOK TWO

LIFE in a Tumble Dryer

Living and Working in Khartoum,
the World's Hottest Capital

LEOMA GILLEY

Copyright © 2024 by Leoma Gilley

Life in a Tumble Dryer
Living in the World's Hottest Capital
Not How I Planned It Memoirs: Book 2

All rights reserved.
No part of this work may be used or reproduced, transmitted, stored, or used in any form or by any means graphic, electronic, or mechanical, including but not limited to photocopying, recording, scanning, digitizing, taping, Web distribution, information networks or information storage and retrieval systems, or in any manner whatsoever without prior written permission from the publisher.

Disclaimer: This book is in part a memoir. It reflects the author's present recollections of experiences over time. Some names and characteristics may have been changed, some events have been compressed, and some dialogue has been recreated from memory. This is a book of memory, and memory has its own story to tell. But it is a truthful story as best memory can provide.

In this world of digital information and rapidly-changing technology, some citations do not provide exact page numbers or credit the original source. We regret any errors, which are a result of the ease with which we consume information.

NO AI TRAINING: Without in any way limiting the author's (and publisher's) exclusive rights under copyright, any use of this publication to "train" generative artificial intelligence (AI) technologies to generate text is expressly prohibited. The author reserves all rights to license uses of this work for generative AI training and development of machine learning language models.

Photos in the book credited to Leoma Gilley unless otherwise noted. All photos used with permission.

Ethiopic Script example obtained by SIL via ScriptSource.org.

An Imprint for GracePoint Publishing (www.GracePointPublishing.com)

GracePoint Matrix, LLC
624 S. Cascade Ave, Suite 201, Colorado Springs, CO 80903
www.GracePointMatrix.com   Email: Admin@GracePointMatrix.com
SAN # 991-6032

A Library of Congress Control Number has been requested and is pending.

ISBN: (Paperback) 978-1-961347-93-9
eISBN: 978-1-961347-94-6

Books may be purchased for educational, business, or sales promotional use.
For bulk order requests and price schedule contact:
Orders@GracePointPublishing.com
Printed in U.S.A

Table of Contents

Introduction 1

Chapter 1: The Arrival...5

Chapter 2: Finding a Home 17

Chapter 3: 1990 75

Chapter 4: 1991 139

Chapter 5: 1992 169

Chapter 6: 1993 217

Chapter 7: 1994 253

Chapter 8: 1995 283

Glossary of Foreign Words 295

References 299

About the Author..301

Introduction

Prior to the stories in this book, I had been living in Sudan for four years: a year in Khartoum learning Arabic, a few weeks in Malakal, and three years in Juba, the regional capital of southern Sudan. My work with SIL International was to understand why the Shilluk people could not read their own language. Literacy materials were scarce, and the Bible Society had translated and published the New Testament in 1968. This version challenged the most fluent readers. I was to discover why they were having a problem. Did they just need literacy materials to teach them to read, or was the writing system inadequate? It sounds simple, but I soon learned that with the Shilluk language, nothing is as it seems.

To communicate with people, I spent eight months learning Sudanese colloquial Arabic, meaning I could speak and understand, but not read or write. Then I needed to learn the Shilluk language. My brief time in a Shilluk village outside of Malakal got me started, but then the civil war began, and I evacuated to Juba, the regional capital. There, I continued to study the language with a few people and eventually ended up in England, studying for a PhD in linguistics. I found Shilluks living in London and continued trying to understand the system of sounds.

After four years and a degree, I returned to Sudan to create a writing system that the Shilluks (a.k.a. Cøllø) could read. I knew more and had ideas, but would the Shilluks accept them? Language and culture are inseparable. The Shilluks are a hierarchical people with a king. The elders held great power in the community, so working from the top down was imperative.

Many Shilluks had fled to northern Sudan because of the civil war that began in 1983. My friends in London kept me abreast of news from Sudan, so I knew that going to Khartoum would be a better option than going to Kenya or Uganda. SIL moved out of Juba, so that was not a choice. The Shilluks and I had taken refuge in the world's hottest capital city, Khartoum.

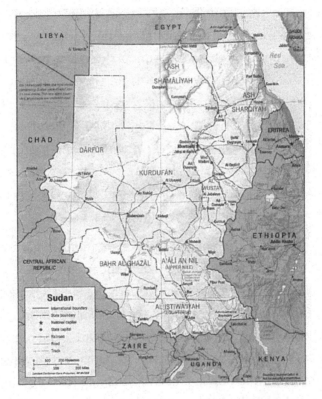

Some names used in these stories have been changed at the request of the individual or their relatives. Where possible, each person mentioned has seen what I've written and approved it, except for those who are no longer with us.

Most of my letters are addressed to my cousin, Harriet. As an only child, Harriet filled in as my older sister. She is the only family member to visit me in Sudan during my 20 years there.

"Shilluk has baffled missionaries, linguists, and anthropologists for many decades. Back in the 1940s and 50s, missionaries tried to write Shilluk and even did some Bible translation. Unfortunately, the language, particularly the sound system, was so difficult that the translations they did are virtually unusable. The alphabet they chose just doesn't make any sense of the language. Leoma, after seven years of extensive research, finally broke into the sound system and has developed an alphabet which is nothing short of a milestone." (Russ Hersman, Personal communication.)

Chapter 1:
The Arrival

Dear Harriet,

When I last wrote, I had moved to London to study for my doctorate degree at the School of Oriental and African Studies (SOAS). The description in England is "reading for a degree" and I read a lot. SOAS has one of the best libraries in the world for African studies. My tutor was excellent, so I was more than prepared for the oral examination. I had two examiners, an internal from the University of London and an external from the Netherlands. I sent off my precious writing to these two men, feeling as if I'd sent my child off to school for the first time. They would evaluate me based on what I had written, and I could not defend or explain it until the day of the oral exam. The main purpose of meeting in person for the examination was to ensure that the author had actually written the thesis. After thirty minutes, they ran out of questions. These exams are normally two hours long. So, I said, "The only person I've had to talk with about this is that man over there [pointing to my tutor]. So, if you have another question, ask me another question!"

The Dutch professor asked me one more question, and when I had answered that, he said, "And that is all!" They dismissed me to the hallway, where I got very nervous. What if they hadn't liked what I had said?

Shortly, my tutor came out to congratulate me, and we all enjoyed a couple of glasses of champagne. Traditionally, PhD students must change something after their exam. I had to change my full stops (periods) in relation to my quotes, a simple task to complete.

I had attended a friend's MA graduation in the Royal Albert Hall a few months before I finished. As I watched innumerable students bowing and curtsying to the Princess Royal, I found my American-ness rising within me. I decided not to curtsy to anyone! So, I skip-ped my graduation and had them mail my diploma.

During my time in England, I not only gained a degree, I also met Janice during her training course. She had taken early retirement from teaching and joined SIL. Her training with SIL was mother-tongue education, or simply, literacy. We got on well, despite her being a few years older. We spent months getting acquainted before she agreed to join me in Khartoum. In August 1988, the day I had my oral examination, she headed to Kenya for an orientation course. We met up in Nairobi in February 1989.

After completing my degree, I spent the rest of the year in the US visiting my supporters and celebrating with my proud parents. I was the second person in my extended family to get a PhD.

Love,

L

Dear Harriet,

In September 1988, the SIL-Sudan Director sent a report about the need to relocate all staff away from Juba. It was a far-reaching and painful decision. He had to leave Nigeria several years before, and this move brought back hard memories. They shipped two of our vehicles to Khartoum for future use there. He gave various other vehicles, the computer, and the printer to the governor's office. They exchanged our Sudanese pounds with other NGOs (non-governmental organization) for US Dollars. Personal effects were sent either to Nairobi, Uganda, or Khartoum.

The director phoned me to ask where I wanted my things to go. The Shilluks lived in the northern part of the southern region, so I said, "Khartoum."

One deciding factor leading to the decision to leave Juba was the demand for our Cessna airplane. On any day, there were thirty or more government officials waiting to fly in our five-seater plane. We didn't know how to set priority on who should fly. Another factor was the limit on grain supplies coming into Juba. The SPLA (Sudan People's Liberation Army) attacked convoys. It could take months before supplies got through. Then, the regional government's influence on the central government in Khartoum weakened. Renewal of our registration was in question. Our residence visas depended on that registration.

From the Khartoum government's point of view, SIL's work in southern Sudan was a threat to the Arabic language. We encouraged the use of local languages, based on a Roman alphabet, and the government saw that as damaging to Islam. Also, our moving around in southern Sudan implied we had ties with the SPLA rebels. These factors led to SIL-Sudan leaving Juba to work in neighboring countries. Our director got the governor's signature on a renewed registration before he departed. How long the central government would allow that to stand was anyone's guess. At least it was a signed document, and that counts for a lot in Sudan.

Love,

L

Dear Harriet,

Knowing what Khartoum was like, I took advantage of products available in the US, purchasing solar panels, solar lights, solar fans (the desktop type) as well as books, clothes, etc. Each extra box above my luggage allowance cost $150, but I considered it an excellent investment. Upon entering Kenya, I didn't want to go through customs with things destined for Sudan, so I put them in storage at the airport.

Janice and I attended our group conference in Limuru, Kenya. It was a great time to see our colleagues, but this conference became known as the "red hankie conference." All our colleagues had evacuated from Sudan and were feeling the pain of loss. Whenever anyone gave a testimony, the same red hankie appeared to wipe away tears. I hope someone washed it in between uses. It was cathartic to experience our sense of loss together. While Sudan is a hard place to live, it seems an even harder place to leave.

After several years in Sudan and studying for my doctorate in England, I had significant changes in my thinking. So, let's explore those.

I mentioned to Wanda, a colleague, that she should change one aspect of the Ndogo language program. That suggestion netted more than I bargained for. She sounded annoyed with me for implying that SHE could change the way things were going. "I can discuss it with them and see what THEY want to do. But it is their language and thus their decision." Little did I realize how often those words would come back to haunt me and caution me against my own paternalistic attitudes.

A few years on, someone wrote to me asking, "Who approved the Cøllø orthography?" The implication was that our experts should have the chance to make sure it met their linguistic standards. My reply was almost as curt as Wanda's. "The Cølløs have agreed on it, and I have no power to change it. It is their language and while I can make suggestions, it is their decision."

I often found myself in situations where I needed to recognize my own limitations. They invited me to act as a consultant, not as the judge of what was right for their language or culture or problem. As outsiders, we can offer suggestions and solutions based on our expertise, but we can't fix it.

Thomas Laku, a Sudanese, wrote his MA thesis on the problem of community participation. He explained the dilemma when he said,

Many times, organizations, both non-governmental organizations and others, enter a country and, after some observation, decide what the people need to improve their standard of living. That "need" can range from a pit latrine to formal education and anything in between. The result is often that the people themselves see the pit latrine, or the education, as something being imposed upon them, which they have no desire to utilize. They are sometimes not consulted as to what they want or need and, if they are left out of the planning process, can feel as if they have only been used to fulfill an organization's goals. This is not participation by the community. The results of this lack of participation are often that the pit latrine, or education, or whatever happens to be the focus, is neglected, cast aside as an undesirable commodity. As a result of this, it is of paramount importance that the local people feel that they are a part of the project from its inception. (Thomas Laku, Personal communication.)

Somewhere along the line, the Shilluks showed me they could understand the issues if presented coherently. They didn't always agree with me or with each other. But their inherent resolve to let everyone have his or her say taught me to keep my mouth closed and just watch and listen.

Love,

L

Dear Harriet,

Janice and I prepared to depart for Khartoum in February 1989. Our first task at Jomo Kenyatta Airport was to reclaim my multitude of boxes from the bond area. It pleased me to find that they were right where I had left them three weeks before. The trolley was gone, but otherwise, they appeared to be in good condition and unopened. The man in charge kept asking if I was sure the Sudan Airplane would fly that night. I assured him that, provided the plane arrived, we would go to Khartoum at 3:20 a.m.

By the time Janice and I combined our things, we had 256 kilograms (564 lbs.) of luggage! Our friend Russ offered to help check us in. He had contacts at Sudan Air from his time as the office manager in Kenya. He convinced the airline agent to agree we would only pay for 100 kilograms of luggage instead of the total amount, a good bargain. Once we paid for our excess baggage, and they sent it to the plane, Janice and I continued through immigration and on to the gate.

We waited and waited, while nothing happened. I took a brief trip to the ladies' room and upon my return, a queue had formed at our gate. I joined the queue, as I learned long ago it was better to get in a queue and then find out what it was for. Janice wasn't in the queue. Next, I noticed several men in the line were wearing yarmulkes. It was rare to see a Jewish traveler going to Khartoum. Then I noticed the signboard at the gate said El Al, the Israeli airline! It turned out that there had been a mix-up and officials had allocated Gate 7 to both Sudan Air and El Al! Talk about mixing oil and water. The security guards for El Al were in a state, radioing the airport authorities and trying to chase away anyone who appeared to be an Arab. In the end, Sudan Air got moved, and I slipped out of the El Al queue and searched for the Sudan Air sign.

By 3:40 a.m., nothing was happening at our new gate. The plane had arrived, but no gate agent was present to begin the boarding process. At 4:00 a.m., the officials explained there was a "technical fault." We learned about 4:30 that the fault was a flat tire. Later, I heard a rumor that the Kenyan authorities would not sell Sudan Air anything on credit, as Sudan didn't pay their debts in a timely fashion. So, the airline had to fly another tire in from Khartoum. I don't know if that was true, but at 5:00 they took us to the 680 Hotel in downtown Nairobi.

On the bus ride to the hotel, Janice and I were sitting in front of a Shilluk man I recognized. He didn't remember me and was surprised when I greeted him in Shilluk. He joined us for breakfast, and we learned he was trying to sell a Suzuki Jeep. We said we were looking for a good car, and months later, we bought his. The details of that purchase will come later.

The 680 Hotel did not have enough empty rooms for an entire planeload of people. They placed some passengers in the available rooms while the rest of us had breakfast and slept in the lobby until a room became available. Janice and I got a room at 9:30 and slept a couple of hours before returning to the airport.

We hurried through the formalities, arriving at the gate once again. As we reached the bottom steps to the plane, the agent instructed us to identify our luggage before they loaded it onto the plane. Janice went on board to save me a seat, and I began pointing out boxes and bags.

Once I got on board, the passenger section was not full. I suspected our things filled the luggage section! Europe was the destination for most passengers, so when we landed in Khartoum, only seven passengers deplaned. My Shilluk friend, John N., helped us get our boxes, etc., onto four trolleys, but kept his distance once we got to the customs desk.

The airport arrival hall in Khartoum was splendid! I couldn't believe my eyes. It was new, half a mile north of the old terminal. Apparently, they built it when aid deliveries for the drought relief were at their height. US engineers left instructions to turn it into a passenger terminal after the relief flights were no longer needed. The officials followed through, and now the terminal was in use. Even the trolleys were new, and they all worked. We thought we must have gotten into the VIP area by mistake.

Getting through immigration and finding our luggage seemed endless. The customs people disapproved of my packing "electronic stuff" together with "personal stuff." They wanted to make me come back later and pay duty on the electronic things. I have to admit, the way I packed was not accidental. Forty-five minutes of negotiation later, they decided I could take my things and go without charge.

They couldn't understand what the solar panels were. I explained again and again that they took the energy from the sun and stored it in batteries. This was a new concept, and they just shook their heads and asked me again.

At one point, an officer wanted to see Janice's money. As she fished under her clothing for her money belt, he became embarrassed and said, "Oh, sorry, sorry, never mind!"

While we negotiated with the customs officials, someone took my suitcases and boxes off the trolley and left them on the floor. Then he made off with the trolley. Janice and I decided this was one of the few international airports where someone would "steal" the trolley and leave the valuables. We commandeered another couple of trolleys and got ourselves and our stuff out to the parking lot.

Love,

L

Dear Harriet,

It was late afternoon when we emerged from the airport to find Wanda waiting for us in the airport parking lot with a Toyota pickup truck. We piled our stuff and ourselves into the truck. Janice offered to ride in the back with the luggage; there was just enough room for her. We headed off to the Manshia section of Khartoum.

As we turned onto the Africa Road, Wanda cautioned me to observe the route we were taking. She explained that after dropping our things at our Manshia residence, we would go to her house in a different part of town for supper. Then we would drive ourselves back home in the dark. There were no road signs, so I had to watch for landmarks. I paid close attention. At the first traffic light, we turned left onto a tarmac road. After half a mile, there was a turn to the right. We followed Middle Road away from the airport, heading east. We passed a series of shops and small businesses that stretched out for half a mile. Suddenly, the tarmac ended, and we "fell off the end of the tarmac." After that, the way became more challenging.

The dirt road turned into a *medaan* or square. It resembled a large, empty, dusty field with tire tracks going in every direction. We went straight across it and continued on a stretch of bumpy dirt road past several houses, around a bend in the road to a large mud puddle. I had not expected a muddy lake in the middle of this desert landscape, but a water pipe had broken. Wanda kept the wheels on the upper ridges and managed not to get stuck. We proceeded around the corner of a prison, wondering if they would stop us from driving by it. They didn't. After passing the prison we came to another *medaan*. This one we crossed at an angle. Ahead, we saw a large white house with a garden of fruit trees along one side. This was to be our home. As we got out of the truck, Janice asked, "How do we know which way to go when we come back?"

Wanda offered this helpful advice. She said, "Just follow the tire tracks." Strange as it may seem, that advice did work. If the tire tracks led into a mud puddle but you couldn't see them coming out on the other side, best not follow them!

The house at Manshia was a triplex, with two apartments downstairs and one upstairs. We had the upstairs. As we headed up the stairs, I noted it was stuffy and hot. There were windows at the second landing that we could open to relieve the stuffiness. At the third landing, we found the door to the flat, as the British call it. The living room/dining room was 20' x 40' with two verandahs opening to the west and to the south. A small, claustrophobic kitchen with little ventilation was on the west side of the house to the left of the dining room. To the east, an alcove led to a hallway and three doors. The middle door opened onto the largest bathroom I'd seen in a while. We could have held a square dance there!

It came complete with a gecko for a pet. The doors on either end of the hallway were bedrooms, both spacious. Ceilings were 10' to 12' high in hopes the hottest air would rise and get away from the inhabitants. All rooms except the bathroom had ceiling fans.

Lifting a water tank to the roof of the Manshia house (Credit: Dennis Dyvig)

Another couple lived in a flat downstairs, but they were out of the country. As regularly happens to us single ladies, no men were around to help us unload our boxes and bags from the truck. So, being the tough, determined women we were, we off-loaded our stuff and hauled it up the stairs into our new home. We had so much luggage getting on the plane, but in the vastness of our new quarters, it only reduced the echo. And so, we had arrived in Khartoum.

Love,

L

P.S. We found our way back home that night in the dark. That I can still give you the directions years later is testimony to the fact that I became a keen observer of my surroundings in those early years.

Chapter 2:
Finding a Home

Dear Harriet,

After a night's rest, Janice and I began sorting our things and figuring out how to live in our new home. Wanda left us the basics: flour, sugar, and milk powder. But we learned that those basic items were not easily available, and we had to struggle to keep ourselves fed. We had arrived on Thursday, and nothing opened on Friday, the Muslim day of prayer.

On Sunday night, we entered one shop just before we "fell off the end of the tarmac." We wandered through the shop to see what was available. I spied a five-pound plastic bag of what appeared to be sugar. I learned from Wanda that the government rationed sugar and almost every necessity of life. We did not have a ration card, as they only issued those on January 1 of any year. Arriving in February proved to be our first major mistake. I casually picked up the bag of sugar and placed it on the counter in front of the shopkeeper. She looked at me oddly and said, "When did you arrive in Khartoum?" I looked back with my most innocent and naïve gaze and said, "Thursday." She smiled and said, "Okay." And with that, she sold us the sugar. That was the only time it happened, but it helped to have made that purchase.

A few days later, our friend Russ and his family moved in downstairs. Russ purchased (possibly on the black market) a fifty-pound sack of flour that we shared. Janice proved to be an excellent shopper and loved to wander through shops, discovering many useful items. I was and am a lousy shopper and grateful not to go shopping.

The only bread items we could find were less than satisfactory. One kind was hard, dry bread akin to melba toast, only thicker. The local bread had no preservatives, so when stale, it got hard enough to use as a weapon. Since it was such a precious and rare commodity, merchants cut the leftovers into thick slices, dried them, and sold them. They were edible if dipped in coffee or something to soften them. Another find is called *shahari*, which means "hair" and is similar to sweet shredded wheat. Then there was the *kisra*, which had the thickness of a thin crepe that crumbles when dry. It tastes tangy since they ferment the batter before cooking. In desperation, we started putting peanut butter and jelly on *kisra*. I don't recommend it. In fact, those moments were our most desperate ones.

Russ and his wife, Lynda, brought their six-year-old daughter with them. Amy was a bit pigeon-toed, and someone had suggested teaching her to roller skate, to train her feet to point straight ahead. That sounded fun and useful, so they brought a pair of roller skates. She skated on the verandah in front of their apartment while the local children looked on with awe.

We had a guard for the compound named Shila. (Some languages don't distinguish between "s" and "sh," so his name was supposed to be Silas but ended up as Shila.) He helped clean the apartments, and his presence provided protection from petty thievery. He and his family lived in a small mud house on the compound.

One day, we saw Saphira, a two-year-old, walking around in the sun (with the temperature at 100°F in the shade), wearing nothing but a pair of white, fur-lined boots. Amy thought those boots were great and begged her parents for a pair. I guess she would have traded in her roller skates had the boots been big enough for her. It just shows: The grass is always greener on the other side.

Love,

L

Dear Harriet,

We had lived in Khartoum in our upstairs apartment for two months when another single woman named Jo arrived. She stayed with us for a few weeks until she found her own place. I tried to orient her to the city and the climate. I told her, "Jo, it's hot in Khartoum."

She said, "Oh, I've been in Juba."

"I've been in Juba too!" I countered, "and Khartoum is hot."

She thought I was exaggerating, but a few days into April, the temperature went up. As we watched the sunset over the verandah one afternoon, she said, "There goes that blazing ball of fire for yet another day. But it will return tomorrow to torment us once again."

Janice is English and loves the sunshine. So, every morning, Janice remarked, "Oh, it's another nice, sunny day!"

If Jo were present, she would say, "Janice, it is NOT a NICE sunny day. The sun is not our friend here!"

While the Manshia flat offered the basics, no Shilluk people lived in that area. Since our work was with the Shilluk, we needed a house near them. In a city of three million people spread across the desert, our location was very important. As we looked for a place to live, we learned several lessons, usually the hard way.

Lesson 1: Top-floor apartments and single-story houses are HOT. The dwelling absorbed the full force of the sun throughout the day. If there was a story above, it shaded the floors below, but for the top, there was no relief. Janice and I often visited our downstairs neighbors just to have a cooler place to go.

Lesson 2: Make sure you live in an area with electricity or buy a generator! Riyad, Amarat (the new extension), and Manshia had a poor supply of electricity. The power company assumed if you owned a house in those parts of town, you could afford a generator. So, when there wasn't enough power to go around, the power board cut off electricity to those areas first. Our Manshia house had a generator.

Lesson 3: There should be a cooling system installed and in good working order before you sign an agreement. There was no air conditioner or air cooler when Jo first moved into her top-floor apartment.

She found the temperature hit 100°F before 10:00 in the morning. Her fans in the apartment only contributed hot air blowing around, which was not conducive to working. In order to concentrate on work, she drove to the American Club and sat near the pool. Once the sun set, she returned home and opened the doors and windows to cool the place down. The walls and ceiling collected heat during the day and gave it off at night. It was quite unpleasant.

One night, as Jo was sleeping under these rigorous conditions, the wind began to blow. At first, this appeared to be a blessing, as the air felt cooler. But, in Khartoum, when the wind blows, look for more than just air. There is also dust. That occasion was a mighty haboob (sandstorm)!

As soon as the haboob began, the power went off so that if the power lines hit together, they would not blow things up. Without electricity, Jo couldn't see the dust. It took time before she touched her face with her hand—and felt the sandy dust. A thick layer of fine dust covered her and everything in her apartment.

Realizing this, she jumped up and closed the windows. This hasty action kept out the dust, but also blocked the breeze, and then the humidity made itself felt. The heat rose, and she broke out into a sweat. Before long, she thought she preferred the dirt to sitting in those sweltering conditions for another minute.

Before Jo could decide what to do, it started sprinkling. It often rained a bit because of the increased humidity and the temperature change. The ground didn't even get wet. I think Texans call it a 12" Texas rain, meaning that the raindrops are 12" apart. The combination of rain and dust created mud. The water came in around her closed windows and mud ran down her walls. After a night of sweltering heat, very little sleep, and listening to the wind howling around her apartment, she awoke to find everything covered in mud or dust. As she was telling us this sad tale, I couldn't help but ask, "Jo, what did you think when you saw that?"

Her memorable remark was, "That was the closest thing to hell I ever hope to experience."

When another couple were looking for a house, an agent told them they didn't need air coolers if they lived in Bahri (North Khartoum) because it was cooler there. The wife asked if someone had put an enormous umbrella over that part of town.

During the next haboob, I was lying on the couch with a stomach complaint. As I looked out the French doors onto the southern verandah, I watched the world turn yellow. I decided the best way to cope with the dust was to make up a song. One came to me and Janice threw in a verse. Here is the outcome. The tune is "The

Yellow Rose of Texas," but this version is "The Yellar Dust of Khartoum."

Oh, the yellar dust of Khartoum,
the likes you never see'd.
It covers like a garment, o'er people, floors, and trees.
It appears in just a moment, but lasts for days and days,
Oh, yellar dust of Khartoum, we truly stand amazed.

When you're walkin' in a dust storm,
you'll think you've lost your mind.
You can't tell where you're going, nor what you've left behind.
The sand gets in your nostrils, your mouth and both your eyes.
And if you stand there long enough, it'll bury you alive.

We have no need of makeup; it rains down naturally.
Face color's only sandstorm brown, but gray from toes to knees.
Your oily skin is daily dried by that abrasive touch,
but one good thing about it, it doesn't cost that much.

My hair is like a pan scrub, my skin is like a beach.
The tub is standing empty; the water will not reach.
There isn't any power, and bread's in short supply.
I chose to go to Khartoum, and now I wonder WHY!

If you own a photocopier, computer, or cassette,
be sure to keep it covered, because if you forget,
the dust will work its magic on every moving part,
and you will bring a job and joy to your repairman's heart.

Oh, the yellar dust of Khartoum, the likes you never see'd.
It covers like a garment o'er people, floors, and trees.
It will tan you in an instant while blocking out the sun.
Oh, yellar dust of Khartoum, this time you've really won!!

Love,

L

Dear Harriet,

While we were looking for a house, we were trying to buy John's Suzuki Jeep. Both efforts proved more difficult than we had imagined, but then Sudan stretches what one can imagine.

We wanted a simple Sudanese-style house at a standard that we could live in but also to encourage Shilluk people to visit. It was important to be near a large Shilluk community. There were two possibilities: south of Omdurman in Fitihab or in Hai Jusef. Hai Jusef had experienced terrible floods in 1988, so we thought Fitihab, on higher ground, might be a better location.

The greater Khartoum is a T-junction where the "roads" are the Niles (shown as lines with the names in boxes). Below is a schematic map.

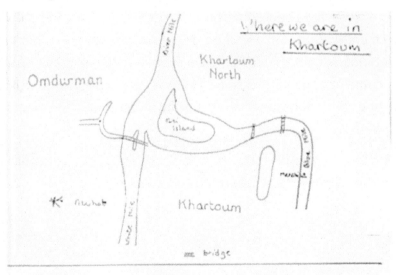

Schematic of Greater Khartoum

We looked at several properties in various parts of the city. Hai Jusef and Fitihab were the two places the Shilluk people lived. The families in Hai Jusef were less well-off and less educated than those in Fitihab. Since we needed people to advise us on the writing system and potential changes, we decided Fitihab was the better choice. The section of Omdurman that we looked in is called *Muhandiseen* (Engineers). One house was three years old and in good and clean condition. They wanted $320/month rent, but that seemed excessive. It had a living-dining room, closed verandah, sitting room, kitchen, three bedrooms and one indoor and two outdoor toilets. In addition, the tiled, flat roof was so large we could have hosted a square dance. The woman offered to leave any furniture we wanted. Other than the immensity of the place, the major drawback was the 8' x 10' garden with no place inside for the car.

Another house was across from the army, with four guards facing it 24/7. It was near the main road, not as isolated as the other homes we had seen. It had a splendid garden with grass, trees, flowering plants, and a parking place with a sunshade over it. There were three bedrooms, two enclosed verandahs, two salons, three bathrooms, and a kitchen. The upwardly mobile owner was a veterinarian who had qualified in Scotland. He had taken care of his home and wanted us to do likewise. We thought our visitors might be uncomfortable with the army monitoring movements at our house.

The home we decided on was 35 km (22 miles) from our office in Manshia. It proved to be a significant distance.

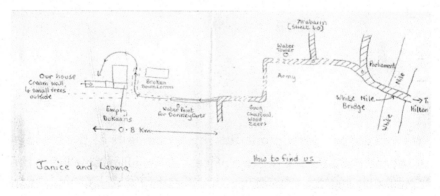

Directions to the Fitihab house from Khartoum

We crossed the old White Nile Bridge and wandered past a huge army barracks. Then we made a 90° turn to the left at the large cement water tower and drove past the second side of the army. After another sharp right-angle turn, we rode over a short bit of paved road before dropping off the end of that tarmac and bouncing along the washboard dirt road. After a few jarring moments, we ended up at a house owned by Mr. Abdul. He was married, with four daughters and one son. Two daughters were studying pharmacology in the Middle East. Najwa, the eldest daughter, knew a little English and enjoyed practicing with us. The fourth daughter was four years old and ruled the household. The son attended secondary school.

Mr. Abdul had taught for several years in the Gulf. The generous salary enabled him to build this house in Omdurman. Since he had not been present to supervise the construction, many of the fittings, such as taps, doors, etc., were of poor quality or badly constructed. They had lived in the house since his return and needed the rent to pay their other bills. They moved to a less grand house three blocks away, and we visited each other often. The only concern for them was leaving behind their three air conditioners, just as summer began. We agreed to buy an air cooler that they could use. When we stopped renting their house, we would reclaim that air cooler. Russ picked up a cooler in the industrial area and took it to their house. They installed it and seemed satisfied.

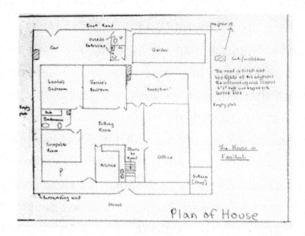

House plans

All the rooms in our new house opened onto a large inner sitting room. There were three bedrooms and two small, enclosed verandahs, one on either side of the house. Most Arab homes have a women's side and a men's side. The women's side is near the kitchen. There was an inside bathroom and, of course, the kitchen. A large salon, which they used as a formal dining room and sitting room, completed the house. Outside the salon and men's verandah was a postage-stamp-sized garden with grass and several bougainvillea. There was an outdoor shower, toilet, storage room, and parking for the car. Inside, a wide staircase with no stair railing led to the roof. The vast expanse of tiled roof proved too windy to sleep, but it was a lovely place to eat our supper and watch the sunset. We observed the locals without being so visible. Mr. Abdul had planted several trees in front and urged us to water them regularly. There was a shop built into the wall beside the house. The back of the shop was locked, so the shopkeeper did not have access to our compound. This became our home for a year.

Leoma and Janice in the living room in Fitihab

Love,

L

Dear Harriet,

Having secured a house, we needed a car as the house was "out in the boondocks!" Janice and I got a mechanic's assessment of John N's Suzuki Jeep, and he thought it was a good car. But it was another matter to gain ownership of it. We needed the title transferred to our names. That sounded like a simple task, but once again, it stretched us.

John N worked for the Sudan Council of Churches (SCC). SCC had imported cars duty-free four years before. Then they sold those cars to their employees. Once the employee completed payment for the car, they could transfer the title, at least in theory. So, John began transferring the title from the SCC to himself. He would then transfer it to us.

John took the car to customs with a letter from SCC saying they were selling him the car. But the customs officer wanted the import license. John assumed they wanted to see SCC's import license. When he brought that, they said, "No, we want YOUR import license." They insisted he go to the Ministry of Commerce to get that document.

He couldn't even find an entrance when he arrived at the ministry. Shilluks often work as gatekeepers, and there was one present at that ministry. He told John of a "secret gate," and as John entered, the gatekeeper said, "Let the son of the king come in." (The Shilluks have a king, and John was from the royal family.) Once inside, the authorities told him to bring a letter from the Ministry of Foreign Affairs, even though John was Sudanese and worked for a Sudanese organization. Off he went to get such a letter. However, as one might expect, the Ministry of Foreign Affairs refused to give him the required letter because he was Sudanese and worked for a Sudanese organization.

John never escaped that endless circle. At that point, he left for a ten-day work trip. That trip took him two weeks. Upon his return, we found him in despair because they had lost the papers he had turned in. Finally, he sold us the car, and we left the title in SCC's name for the next five years.

The day we drove the Suzuki home to Manshia, the director asked if we would trade it for the year-old Toyota Corolla he had recently purchased. The deal sounded suspicious, so I asked him why. It turned out that the diplomat illegally brought in the Corolla for his wife. The embassy allowed one car per household, but this guy had brought in a second car. He paid no duty, and the embassy was having nothing to do with it. The diplomat and his wife had left the country, so we couldn't return the car, and the paperwork ended up in limbo. The director could keep the car but never sell it, as there was no way to pay the duty or transfer the title. We did not make the trade!

Leoma in the Suzuki

I've blown you away enough for today, so more tomorrow.

Love,

L

Dear Harriet,

In order to drive our car, we needed Sudanese driver's licenses. Here was another opportunity to learn to cope with the local bureaucracy.

Rauf, one of our Sudanese employees, took us to get our driver's licenses. Before we traveled to Sudan, we had each gotten an international driver's license. By using the international license, we hoped to avoid testing. We arrived at the office that dealt with driver's license paperwork. The first order of business was to buy a file folder from a small boy. We missed that cue. But Rauf knew our papers must be in a file folder to be accepted. It was supposed to help them organize their filing system.

After purchasing the folders, we approached the first window. The man spoke very good English and explained everything that we needed to do. When we finished there, he told us to go to the next window. As we stepped to the neighboring window, he changed places with the man behind the desk at that window. I guessed the second man didn't know enough English to communicate with us, so he saved everyone trouble by switching places. Once again, he instructed us as to what we should do at that desk. Then he told us to move across the way to the next window.

As we stood in this third queue, we learned they had added a new form to the long list of required forms. Rauf helped us fill out this new form in Arabic. After that, we received temporary licenses until they issued proper ones.

We used these licenses for several years.

Love,

L

Dear Harriet,

Janice had sent a barrel of things to Khartoum from Manchester airport. In early March 1989, a telex arrived to tell us it was now in Khartoum. Rauf checked on it and reported that customs had "put it in prison." Janice went to the firm handling the barrel on March 30. She wrote a list of the contents without stating the values and they told her to return "sometime." Rauf said she should go back on April 1. She was maneuvering the Toyota pickup into place when the engine died and refused to restart. After two and a half hours, they asked her to come back on April 3, so she took a taxi home. Russ got the Toyota working again and drove it back to Manshia.

Janice dropped by to see John N regarding the car papers on the 3rd. When she exited his house, she had a flat tire. Since she was supposed to pick up the barrel, she took a taxi. The manager of the freight company was having car trouble as well, so she got his sympathy. She kept wondering how she would get this barrel home! In the end, she had to pay $25, which included the customs duty and handling charges. The manager then said, "Our lorry will take you and the barrel home." The customs people had gone through her things with a fine-tooth comb, but nothing was missing. We were delighted to have an electric kettle.

Love,

L

Dear Harriet,

In April 1989, Janice received an invitation to attend a Coptic wedding. She arrived at the same time as the bride. They lavishly decorated the car with looped ribbon and announced its arrival several streets away by blowing the horn. The bride wore a beaded, white satin dress with hoops and a train. She carried a white feather fan and a bouquet of red roses. The chief bridesmaid wore a beaded pink dress. There were several girls and two boy attendants. The women greeted the bride's arrival with loud ululations. Janice sat outside the church by the back door with a good view down the aisle. Many people crowded to the door when the bride entered on her brother's arm. A Sudanese neighbor said, "We can't see here, let's go inside." They moved to the front side door and took seats inside in the fourth row! After the bride entered, servers handed out favors and sweets on small metal trays covered in net.

They decorated the church with a large floral heart and palm fronds and bougainvillea along the side walls. The bride and groom, best man, chief bridesmaid, and three clergymen sat on decorated seats on the platform. The audience could see the beautiful henna designs on the bride's and bridesmaids' hands and feet. As is the custom, the bridegroom had henna on his knuckles and ends of his fingers. Janice felt distinctly underdressed. Silver and gold lamé net and sequins were much in evidence among the guests. The men wore suits. It was a lively occasion. The choir sang six times, the congregation not at all. There was a brief speech in English, interpreted into Arabic. They asked the speaker to hurry as he had overrun his time! One of the readings was from Ruth. A Coptic clergyman appeared halfway through the ceremony. After the exchange of vows, he blessed the couple, embraced the other clergy, and left.

The chief bridesmaid used the feather fan to cool off the bride at intervals. A professional videographer captured the whole thing on film. He and his attendant light carrier were highly visible throughout the ceremony. There was a lovely atmosphere of fellowship and oneness. After signing the register, the couple left, preceded by bridesmaids throwing rose petals. Then the guests mingled and chatted. There were Copts and Muslims. The Muslim men were in white *jalabiyas* and turbans, the women in *tobes*. The Muslims sat outside the church.

The congregation proceeded to the Coptic Club for an outdoor reception for approximately five hundred people. There was a five-tier cake along with plates of *tahini* and *babaganoush*, a dip made with eggplant. This was followed by beef similar to Wiener schnitzel and then pieces of chicken. Servers provided Pepsis for everyone since alcohol is illegal in Sudan.

The bride and groom started dancing, and soon others joined them. Attendees sat at tables for eight and visited back and forth. Janice talked with a Shilluk family, and later met the husband, children, and grandchildren of a woman she had seen at church the previous Sunday. At midnight, Janice left for home. One nice thing in Sudan is that leaving early doesn't offend anyone. They are just sad to see you go.

Love,

L

Dear Harriet,

Having secured a car, a driver's license, and a house, it was moving day. In early May, Janice and I moved our two kittens and our meager possessions to our new enormous house. Our only possessions were: a card table and two folding chairs, two beds and my two cedar boxes that I evacuated from the village near Malakal. We found nothing broken as we unpacked the glasses and other items that were stored in these chests.

We needed a few more chairs, so we hastened to the furniture shops on Sharia Arbayiin (40th Street) to search for something that looked comfortable and was in our price range. There were two chairs with metal tubing for the frame, metal slats in the seat and back, and foam cushions. Chairs came in sets of four or six, to be placed in a rectangular pattern around a coffee table. Somewhere along the way, two people bought only three or five chairs, leaving behind two different, individual chairs. One was brown and the other was light green. The storekeeper couldn't sell them since they weren't in a set because no one in their right mind wanted just one. So, when two foreign women showed interest in these two odd chairs, he was eager to get rid of them. We got a good price, but as we prepared to shove them into the car, the shop-keeper became alarmed. "Had we noticed they were different?"

"Yes."

He placed them side by side and pointed out the different colors and styles. Yes, we saw that. In the end, we had to assure him we would put them in different rooms before he allowed us to take them home.

Our next major buy was in the Omdurman market. We decided we needed more than two odd chairs, so we looked for a full matching set. We found chairs painted silver with round tubes instead of slats at the seat and back. In order to have enough padding, we ordered cushions made with extra cotton stuffing. We purchased several small tables, an essential for any Sudanese household. When a visitor arrived, it was important to serve water or tea. The hostess placed the drink on a table near the right hand of the guest so they could reach their refreshment. We bought a coffee table to put in the center of our sitting room, around which we placed our six chairs.

Once we had furniture, our days took on a rhythm: cleaning, wash-ing dishes, painting, sorting, cleaning, repairing broken windows, installing the solar system, cleaning, washing clothes and dishes, ironing, and watering plants and trees. We visited the neighbors and received an average of five visitors a day. You may have no-ticed that cleaning occurred multiple times in our activities. It seemed as if half the Sahara blew through the house every few minutes. We swept up three to four dustpans full of dirt DAILY from just one room. It became imperative that we find house help!

Our next task was to paint. We followed Russ and Lynda's exam-ple, painting our house ourselves. Our Sudanese visitors thought we had lost our minds! In Sudanese society, women never paint. Labor was a small portion of the cost, so it was more economical to hire a painter. Paint was the expensive part. We learned the hard way, and when we moved to our next house, we took advantage of the excess of day laborers and paid a man to do that job.

Russ painting their flat in Manshia

Our Shilluk contacts recommended a woman named Acwil to work as a house helper. She was a widow and mother of five. Her home was far away, but she still arrived early in the morning. She attacked the dirt like "Mrs. Clean" and soon shined and polished everything. By 10:00 a.m., she completed her chores and lay down in our spare room to take a nap. Once we ate breakfast, she washed the dishes. She did everything except laundry. In her house, everyone washed his or her own by hand. We were working by that time, and we believed laundry was her job. In the end, she left us, but we didn't know why. She came by to visit a few months later and discovered that we had purchased a washing machine. Then she told us how much she hated doing laundry by hand.

Love,

L

Dear Harriet,

After a ten-hour day, we happily sat in our garden near the cool grass, crepe myrtle, roses, and orange daisies. It was 102°F in the house at the end of May, and there was a power cut from 2:30 to 4:30. We were without water several times a day, but when it came on, we took showers and cleaned up the kitchen.

We had several odd taps in the bathroom that stuck out of the wall. If we turned one tap, a trickle of water flowed into the bidet below it. If we turned the other one, water spewed from the pipes in the wall. The plumbing could be in the Ripley's Believe It or Not! museum. I discovered copper wire in the fuse for my air conditioner!

The Swiss embassy gave a demonstration on how to use solar ovens. They cooked an entire meal in them on the roof of the embassy. We decided to purchase one since they didn't cost that much, and we had plenty of sun. The solar oven is a wooden box about 3' square on short legs. Inside has a metal surface on the bottom and sides. The bottom is painted black to absorb heat. The top comprises two panes of glass with half an inch of space between them. They have a wood frame that is hinged to the top and the lid. The plywood lid had another metal sheet on the inside. A 2' wooden stick holds the lid open during cooking. The idea is to put a pan with a black lid on top of two pieces of wood in the bottom to allow the heat to surround the pot. Lower the glass cover over it and position the metal part of the lid to catch the sun and reflect the light into the cooker. One day, we prepared our rice, then added leftovers. We nearly burned the vegetables. Since electricity is unpredictable, and gas bottles are often difficult to fill, this provides an excellent alternative. It is slow, but sure.

Leoma with the solar cooker

By June 1989, summer had arrived. Temperatures reached 100°F in the house and 120°F in the shade in the afternoons. With air conditioners on full blast, we could get the room temperature to 80°F, if we had electricity. Janice and I often sat on the roof in the evening to enjoy the cooler breeze. But dust storms came suddenly, and we had to beat a hasty retreat inside. Our teeth were gritty, our skin had dust-colored makeup, and we had no power. We would sit drenched in sweat in a dust-filled room. That's living the life in Sudan.

Love,

L

Dear Harriet,

Once we moved out of the Manshia apartment, SIL set it up as the office for Khartoum. The administration rented a house with a telephone line. However, it took a year and a half to get the wire extended into the house with a telephone at the end. After it arrived, it worked for two months and then died.

Denny, our administrator, struggled for another two years to get a working phone. He bought wire, paid overtime, and made frequent trips to the telephone office. Our sponsoring agency wrote many letters asserting that we needed this telephone. Finally, we got a local line. That meant we could phone people in the city. While we could not make international calls, we received calls from outside the country.

He realized the phone bill was due when he picked up the receiver and the line was dead. The quickest way to restore service was to go to the telephone company to pay the bill. But even paying our bill was not straightforward.

Most offices had international lines, so the phone company decided that our office must have one too. Every few months, they gave us an enormous bill for the "international calls" we had supposedly made. The member of staff paying the bill reminded them we only had a local line, so there could be no international calls. At that point, the amount we owed dropped. When he paid that modest charge, they restored service.

Homes rarely had phones. One of my colleagues rented a house with an international line. They let me use it, but I remember sitting for hours waiting for my parents to call me, or worse yet, trying to get through to them.

Have you thought about how life would be if you were unable to telephone someone? If you got lost in a city of five million, how would you find your way home? Without a phone, you keep driving, using up that precious three-gallon allotment of fuel. Or you find someone you can communicate with and ask them. The helpful person might send a small child with you to point the way if your destination were within walking distance. If we had an appointment and something came up, we had no way of letting them know we weren't coming! We just didn't show up. What if there were a family emergency in your home country? How could they let you know? Letters take two weeks and there was no email. If someone got arrested and taken to the police station, it was a challenge to let others know where they were. Thankfully, that didn't happen often! Yes, life without a phone was difficult.

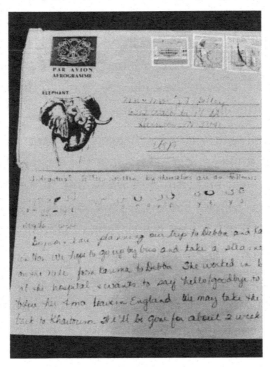

An air form

Church served as an important meeting place. After the service, everyone tried to meet anyone with whom they might have business. We set up appointments, discussed plans, and did most of our networking for the week on Sunday evenings. Once phones were commonplace, services returned to meeting with God instead of with everyone else!

Love,

L

———————

Dear Harriet,

We had interesting neighbors. Our next-door neighbor was a colonel in the army. We visited the family twice but decided not to align ourselves with anyone in the military. The family had barbed wire around the top of their outer wall, as we did. But, on one of our visits, I noted that even the children examined the wire to see if anyone had attempted to breach it. I thought they were paranoid.

A Nuer woman with five or six children lived across the road. Her husband was studying somewhere. Martha dropped by to borrow some tea or sugar and visit for a while. She spoke no English, so Janice was glad when I could translate for her. We learned from her that individual tea bags translated to "selfish bags" in Arabic. Drinking tea is a community act.

On one occasion, she arrived wearing a *tobe*, but once in the house, she took that off, revealing her nightdress. She sat in one of our new chairs in her nightgown, knitting, pulling the yarn from somewhere in her bosom. Martha became fascinated with the counted cross-stitch that Janice and I enjoyed doing, and asked to learn. So, we taught her. Handling the needle was no problem, but she never got the hang of the X. Instead, she made the stitches parallel or at right angles, but not in an X shape. In the end, she gave up.

Our closest neighbor was a photographer who rented the shop in a part of our compound. He painted the outside doors bright red, green, blue, and yellow. The windows held examples of wedding photos he had taken. He helped us by watering the trees. We left the front gate open when he was there so he could go to the back garden for water and to use the outside toilet. Janice chatted with him one day and discovered he was unhappy with his housing. Janice asked why. He explained he was sharing a room with a horse.

In the evenings, men gathered at the shop to visit and watch football (soccer) on a small television. One evening, as we sat in our little garden at the back of the house, a strange man walked up, greeted us, and went into the outside toilet. As he came out, he spoke to us once more and left. We closed the gate for the evening!

We got to know one other family well. Dr. Selma, a kidney specialist, taught at the university while her husband, Hatim, was a pharmacist. They had two small children, a girl and a boy, just beginning school. The government allowed few imports at this time, so the pharmacy business was slow. As a result, Hatim took up serious gardening. Their home was beautiful, and the garden was stunning. Hatim surrounded beds of flowers with hibiscus, palm trees, and roses. The flower beds sometimes filled the whole yard with every color imaginable! At other times, we found the beds covered in luxurious green grass. Selma told us Hatim collected the flower seeds, dried them, and placed them in small plastic bags with labels. The next season, he planted them. If a blossom drooped, it landed in the weed pile before you could say "Scat!"

It was great fun to visit them in the afternoons for tea. We should have practiced our Arabic, but ended up speaking English most of the time because we enjoyed each other's company so much.

We enjoyed our new residence and getting to know our neighbors. But I had to teach in England during the summer, so we added another Sudanese family to our household to keep Janice company. More of that soon.

Love,

L

Dear Harriet,

In the past, the families arranged marriages. While that still happens, more often the man and woman find each other and then tell the parents. Najwa, our landlord's daughter, met a young doctor while studying at the university. They contrived to meet in various public places and maybe in not-so-public ones. They decided to get married, but he had a job offer in Saudi Arabia.

He had to meet Abdul and the family before he left. We visited on the very night the groom's family planned to "drop by." Najwa had been baking cakes and cookies all day for the event to show she knew how to cook. Once his family met Najwa's family, they could ask permission for her to marry their son. That meeting was positive, so they proceeded with plans for the wedding.

The doctor was obliged, as are most Arab men, to give gifts to his bride-to-be. Abdul told us the groom had to send her twelve sets of clothing (from the skin out to the *tobe* she wears to cover herself in public), and a twelve-place-setting of china and silverware along with gold jewelry. She took this to their new home, but it belonged to HER, not to THEM. That meant if the marriage failed, she kept it. The gold jewelry would provide security for her in a less than secure world.

Najwa and the doctor were married, at least on paper, long before the wedding. The doctor and Abdul signed the marriage certificate ahead of time to enable Najwa to get a visa for Saudi Arabia after the ceremony. The bride doesn't sign the license, her father or male relative has to do that.

Love,

L

Dear Harriet,

A Muslim wedding in Khartoum lasts for three days. The first day is the *henna* party. A relative hosts the occasion where the bride receives an extensive henna treatment, decorating her hands and feet with delicate designs. She has a manicure with each nail painted in three different colors. To set the henna and infuse her skin with the scent, she takes a *dukhaan* or smoke treatment with charcoal and sandalwood incense. As long as the henna shows, she doesn't do any housework. The groom has his fingertips done as well as a round spot in the palm of his hand. I'm told this may relate to the god Aton or Aten, the sun god in Egypt. The Nubians of Sudan descend from the Pharaonic peoples and believe Aton will protect them. They invite extended family and close friends to this occasion, which takes place during the daylight hours.

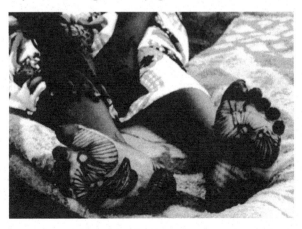

Henna designs for the wedding

Najwa invited Janice and me to her henna party. They greeted us warmly and took us to one of the inner rooms to sit. Since we were the only foreigners attending this affair, they assumed we didn't speak Arabic. We sat near a chest freezer and every few minutes, a woman came by, greeted us, opened the freezer, removed something, and headed to the kitchen. I didn't look in the freezer, take anything out, or go to see how many people were in the kitchen. But, for the hour we watched, at least ten women did. In the end, we joined other guests to converse. The nice thing about Sudanese occasions is that we could do whatever we wanted to. We might lie down on a bed and sleep, sit under a tree or on the verandah and gossip, or help prepare and serve the meal. It was a very easy atmosphere.

The second day, the bride spends the WHOLE day at the coiffeur for a complete body and hair makeover. This service is part of the wedding dress package deal. You may recall seeing the dress shops on Street 15, filled with dazzling white gowns to fulfill any girl's dream. There is no expectation that she buy her dress, since she only wears it once! Instead, she rents it for the night. It is not cheap, but more practical than purchasing one. The shopkeeper requires a gold bracelet as security until she returns the gown the following morning.

Around 8:00 or 9:00 in the evening, she dons her dress and floats to the street where the groom is waiting with the car. The groom arranges for a white sedan to collect his bride. When the car arrives at the shop, decorators descend upon it, armed with multiple rolls of pastel-colored ribbon. They form the ribbon into small loops and fasten them to the hood, top, and sides of the car. The driver progresses in a stately manner to the party with the couple in the back seat. He toots his horn along the way to announce the pending arrival.

A huge crowd awaits the couple. These events are outside at one of the many clubs in the city. There is often a band, though Islamic law forbids men and women dancing or even sitting together in public. The weddings I attended were not so strict and there was modern hip-hop music and typical Sudanese songs.

In a Sudanese dance, the women move only the neck and head sensuously, though sometimes other parts of their body sway. The man never touches the woman, but steps to the music and, if pleased with the woman's performance, snaps his fingers in her direction to show his approval.

The bride, groom, and cameraman at a wedding

This night includes anyone the couple has ever known, often with five hundred to one thousand people in attendance. No one minded if I brought friends. The more the merrier! They offered each person a boiled egg, a piece of bread, French fries, falafel, a bit of feta cheese, a sweet pastry, and a soda. It is best to eat before you attend if you are hungry. The main meal of the day is a delicious lunch for close family and friends. At a wedding lunch in Sinnar, they served roast lamb and lots of other wonderful things!

People talk or visit with friends or relatives while listening to the band. Once the car arrives, the video camera takes over. The couple come in, surrounded by their closest friends. The video camera records their every movement. When the band strikes up their favorite song, they dance while everyone marvels at the beautiful bride. No details get missed by the camera. Then the happy couple moves to the place of honor where they receive their guests.

These wedding seats may include flashing lights in the shape of hearts with red velvet cushions. They are eye-catching. Through the rest of the evening, guests make their way to the couple to offer their congratulations. The video camera records most of them. If things slow down, the cameraman moves through the crowd, from table to table, capturing everyone's presence on film. It is important to be on this video as there is no guest book and the couple will want to know who attended their wedding. After the festivities, visitors get to see these videos. They never grow tired of watching them.

Love,

L

Dear Harriet,

While house hunting, I was working on several linguistic projects. First, I wanted to turn my PhD thesis into a book. I worked on two papers I planned to present at linguistic conferences in Europe. Another colleague wanted to present his paper, so I helped him.

I wrote an explanation of the spelling changes that we needed to make. Five elders considered the suggestions and responded favorably. They suggested that several workshops be run to explain these ideas to a larger group of people after I returned from teaching in England.

Another paper described the steps needed for the literacy project. When our friend John (of car fame) saw this write-up, he suggested writing a formal proposal on behalf of the Shilluk community. A proposal allowed us to seek funds for holding the workshops and printing the materials. We wanted the people to own this, and this was a great start.

Love,

L

Dear Harriet,

Now I will continue with the housing saga. Pastor Peter and his wife, Rachel, had worked with me in Kenya. They moved to Khartoum. We visited them at their rooms on the church compound. Peter and Rachel and their four children stayed in one small room, sharing a bathroom with five other families. It was late April, and the weather had turned hot. The children were listless and bored.

I planned to be away for two months, so Janice and I invited the family to stay at our house. They occupied the large salon, the back verandah, the garden, and the outside bathroom. Rachel set up a kitchen between the outside wall and the side of the house. There was no roof, but then it didn't rain often. It was shady except at midday.

The whole family enjoyed the extra space our home provided. The kids opened the gate for us when we needed to move the car in or out. Peter made a wonderful guard, as he was 6'8". He helped us finish our painting and put up the solar panels. With his height, he reached things we couldn't even see.

Peter and his family had never lived in Khartoum. They came from Malakal, 500 miles south of Khartoum. So, things were as new for them as they were for Janice. We learned together. For example, one evening, Janice and I sat on the roof having dinner. Since Peter and his family were in the garden, it was the next best spot to go to "get away from it all." We finished supper while enjoying the scenery and the cool breeze. I was writing a letter on the computer and as I collected my thoughts, I noticed the neighbor's fluorescent light looked fuzzy. I started to say, "Look at that light" when the cause of the fuzz reached us. It was a haboob. The wind and dust howled around us, blowing everything around the roof. I slammed the computer shut and dashed for the door to go inside. Janice and I returned to the roof, but Janice could barely hold the door open against the wind. She is 5'9" and not petite. I wore contact lenses, so I didn't dare open my eyes very much. I grabbed the folding table, the chairs, and the bedding. My pillow had blown to the far side of the roof.

Once we collected our things, we closed the door and descended to the inner sitting room. The heat rose along with the humidity, with the house closed up. It felt like a sauna. Peter and his family had gone to bed before the storm, so we wondered how they were faring. It was a miserable night.

The next morning, we heard sounds of sweeping and cleaning on the "Shilluk" side of the house. We saw the children out washing our car and sweeping the yard. Peter and Rachel came over and asked, "What happened last night?" They had gone to bed with the windows open, enjoying the cool breeze. In the morning, the dust lay everywhere, and it appalled them.

We had our windows closed, but our side of the house was not much cleaner. We learned how to manage a haboob: Put electronics such as tape recorders, printers, and computers in a closed cupboard, and open the windows and let in the dust. Why fight it when we have no hope of winning?

I get the same question whenever I bring my camera or tape recorder home to be repaired. "Where has this been?!"

"Why?" I asked.

"It was full of sand!"

Love,

L

Dear Harriet,

We enjoyed having Pastor Peter, Rachel, and the family share our home, but our landlord did not approve. He pressured us to have these southerners move out. It took them several weeks to find a place to rent. One of Peter's friends mentioned he had to leave his home, just a few blocks away, because the cost was too high. Peter checked and found that both the house and the rent suited him well. They moved in November. We were glad they stayed in the neighborhood so we could visit.

Rachel mentioned she had a relative who needed a job. As a result, Acol came to work as our house help and stayed for the next fifteen years. She cleaned the house well, but she loved to iron and to cook. How anyone in their right mind enjoyed ironing when it was over 100°F in the shade was beyond me, but Acol loved it. If I couldn't find her, I headed to the back porch where she was ironing on a metal table with sweat pouring from her face. She was always singing.

Love,

L

Dear Harriet,

Our director had warned me that, in Khartoum, living and solving problems would take at least 60 percent of our time. Our work time would be very limited. It took years for us to turn that percentage around in favor of work.

We bought three one-gallon tins of car oil in June 1989. We changed the oil in our Suzuki every six months because the dust and heat were so destructive to the engine. In July, we changed the oil using the first gallon. By August, we noticed there was no oil available in the shops. Stacks of cardboard boxes advertised oil, but when we raced to the shop to buy it, the boxes were empty.

Cars broke down and everyone complained they couldn't get motor oil. We heard the less reputable garages put cooking oil in the engine, disguised as motor oil. It did not stay disguised for long. After the driver took the car a mile away, the engine seized up. This caused more damage than if the motor oil had run out.

After six months of this shortage, we needed another oil change. We thought long and hard, but decided to go ahead. "Surely we could buy more oil soon." Another five months passed, and we had to decide whether to use our last gallon of oil. Suddenly, the market was awash in motor oil. We stocked up again. There wasn't another shortage of that duration, but in Sudan, we never knew. This lesson taught us to keep a good supply of any essentials.

There were many other shortages during that time. Our friend Jo went on vacation. When she returned, she discovered the gas bottle had leaked and was now empty. There was no gas for sale unless one had contacts on the black market, which she did not. The only thing in her house to cook with was a single electric ring. Unfortunately, her electricity was often off for twenty-two hours a day, as it was at our house. She had no way to boil water for coffee. But Jo was not to be defeated. Famous for her creativity, she up-turned two buckets and placed the grill from the gas cooker on top of the buckets. Then she lit three candles underneath and put her coffee pot on top. It took a long time, but the water boiled and she drank her coffee.

One might ask why she didn't use charcoal. She lived on the top floor of an apartment building and the verandah was like an oven while the wind blew a gale most of the time. She refused to stand in the sun and risk being blown away. I guess the candles were just easier.

She sent her gas bottle on a truck to Port Sudan for a refill. It returned six months later—still empty. It was a year before supplies of bottled gas normalized. We kept several bottles in stock to guard against such an occurrence at our house. This particular problem never happened again, but we learned to be prepared.

Love,

L

Dear Harriet,

I attended All Souls church in London while I was teaching in England. Richard Bewes, the rector, had grown up in East Africa. He found out I worked in Sudan when I first arrived at the church at the beginning of my PhD studies. He told me his parents had often hosted workers from Sudan and reminded him to "honor those people. They are in a very difficult place." So, his invitation was to come and rest. Let them care for me. When I felt ready to take part, I would be welcome, but until then, just rest. Oh, how I needed that. So, when I came back for a visit, I received a warm welcome.

John Stott often preached at All Souls, and his words challenged me to draw closer to God. It was easier, more natural, to enter God's presence in England. God seems so close, aware of me, open and welcoming. Perhaps that's because I'm freer to listen and to be with Him. I sense him as the Shepherd, delighted to hold and cuddle his lamb (me), to take my burdens upon Himself, and set me free to walk in his steps. His smile is so gentle, loving, accepting and full of joy that I'm there with Him. It's a real incentive to return often to that lovely peaceful meadow—to be in his presence. It has such a healing effect on my soul. Someday, I must try to describe it, but for now, it's too rich and powerful for mere words to convey. Most blessed is that He shows me that He keeps those things dearest to me next to his heart, to receive his special attention.

While I was in England, Janice ran into challenges. She headed off to meet Jo for breakfast at the Hilton one Friday morning. As she drove up to the White Nile bridge, a soldier flagged her down and told her to turn around. She obeyed, drove to the end of the road, circled the roundabout, and tried once more to cross the bridge. The soldier turned her back. Since she couldn't cross the bridge, she drove to Marian's house and told her what had happened. Marian had listened to the news and explained there had been a *coup d'état*. Janice returned home and stayed there for a few days until things settled.

The National Islamic Front (NIF), headed by Dr. Hassan al-Turabi, joined forces with radical Islamist army officers to seize power from Sadiq al-Mahdi on June 30, 1989. (Werner et al., 526.) At once, everything became more difficult. There was a huge push to implement Islamic law throughout the country and to create an Islamic state. Foreign currency had to be deposited in local banks.

It was a capital offense if the government found you with foreign currency after three months. They executed at least one Sudanese national. All transfers of car titles stopped, thus ending, for a time, our hope of having the title to our car in our names. The implications for the country were much greater, but my purpose is not to explain Sudanese politics. There are other books that focus on that time period. I want to document the practical results of this transition.

Janice had little foreign currency when the coup happened, but other friends had more. Someone hid money in the house because they thought the new government wouldn't last. Others were not so optimistic and opened bank accounts to deposit their money. There was so much distrust of banks that wealthier Sudanese built safe rooms in their homes to secure their money.

I was away during these events, but upon arriving at the airport, the officials sent me to the currency desk to declare my money. I had to list the cash and traveler's checks separately. Upon completion, they drew a squiggle through the rest of the page so I couldn't add something in later. Sometimes they asked to see the money, other times they were too busy.

The exchange rate changed dramatically. A business or embassy exchanged one dollar for four and a half Sudanese pounds (£s4.500). An individual could exchange a dollar for twelve Sudanese pounds (£s12.000). Exchanging money on the black market was possible. The rate was seventy-five Sudanese pounds (£s75.000) to the dollar. But, if the authorities caught that person, it might mean his or her life.

Our car battery died during that time, and the replacement cost was £s4,500 (four and a half thousand pounds). That meant if we were a business, it would cost us $1,000 to buy one car battery. For individuals, a new battery cost $500. It was $60 on the black market. We ordered a new battery from Kenya and had it flown to

Khartoum and filled with acid. Even paying overweight on the plane was cheaper than $500, and safer than exchanging money on the black market.

Love,

L

Dear Harriet,

Another major change to our lives was fuel rationing. In order to buy fuel each week, we were required to choose a particular station. Our day was Monday to receive the allocated ration for that week. (We usually got five gallons, but it might be less.) If we didn't go, or they ran out of fuel, or the generator broke, we had to wait until the next week! They designated one station in town for "make-ups," but I never knew where that was. We used a station near the office since it opened early in the morning. The stations in Omdurman opened later, meaning we queued in the scorching sun. We didn't have to worry about dying of heat stroke at 4:30 a.m. If we were away, someone at the office could collect our ration for us.

We got into the routine of spending Sunday nights with Jo, getting up at 4:00 a.m. with the muezzin's call to prayer and heading out for the petrol station. Two of us filled the two cars. The third person slept in until 6:00 a.m., then bought a large quantity of Egyptian beans and bread for breakfast. People going to the petrol queue took a pillow, a thermos of coffee and something to read. Queues formed just after 4:00 a.m., but it took ten to fifteen minutes of bouncing over the washboard dirt roads to get to the station from Jo's house. By that time, we were fiftieth in the queue and couldn't see the station. We napped until the sun came up, then drank our coffee and read until we reached the pump. The station opened at 6:00 a.m.

Once the fuel was in the tank, we met at Jo's house for breakfast. Egyptian beans are the traditional Sudanese breakfast food, and the only way to get bread. We didn't know how to fix the beans so they were edible. Instead, we poured catsup on them and ate as many as we could stand. I'm ashamed to say it, but we dumped the rest of the beans and wrapped the bread in plastic to keep it fresh. That was the bread we had for the rest of the week.

Love,

L

Dear Harriet,

More regulations came into effect with the coup. In order to get fuel, we had to have a ration card; to get a ration card, we had to have car insurance papers. We needed the title to the car to get insurance papers. SCC still held the title, and transfers of titles had stopped. Now we were in one of those dreaded circles of bureaucracy.

The first week this edict came into force, Janice had to face the man at the gas pump alone. After several hours in the queue, she reached the pump. The man asked for her ration card, which, of course, she didn't have. She burst into tears, explaining, in English, that she had no card but was desperate and what was she to do? The gas station attendant spoke no English, but the message was clear. Men never know what to do with a woman in tears. So, he said "Ma'aleesh" (sorry, nevermind) and put five gallons of fuel in the tank. The next Saturday night, she picked me up from the airport and, while driving to Jo's, told me her sad tale. She ended it by saying, "And I can't cry there again! You have to go this time!"

On Monday morning, I sat in the queue planning my strategy. I got to the pump, and the attendant asked for my ration card. I jumped out of the car babbling in Arabic, "I just got back into the country! There's a new government and new rules. I don't know what to do!" I ranted on, my voice getting higher and higher and more panicked. The man took pity on me, said "Ma'aleesh," and put five gallons in the tank. I thanked him and breathed a sigh of relief.

Later that day, we got the last piece of paper we needed from SCC that enabled us to get the ration card! The following Monday, we went together to the station and when we got to the pump, we both jumped out, waving our ration book. The man recognized us as he didn't have too many excitable foreign women patronizing his establishment. He smiled that we had our ration book, grateful he was no longer liable to get into trouble for giving out fuel.

Love,

L

———

Dear Harriet,

I've mentioned that many commodities were scarce in Khartoum. Well, let me elaborate on that. When I returned from England, we had problems getting not only fuel but also sugar, flour, laundry soap, bread, and tea. Electricity was always a problem with cuts lasting 22 hours. That meant the power was on for two hours a day, often in the middle of the night. We jumped out of bed when the lights came on to turn on the washing machine, print out work done during the day, boil the kettle, and iron until the power shut off again. Then we returned to bed for more sleep.

We discovered we could shop in the Duty Free shop located outside the airport, using our hard currency. They had imported products as well as 50 lb. sacks of sugar. I had British pounds from England, so we spent it to stock up on food within the three months allowed by the government to keep hard currency. The Duty Free was the size of a 7-11 shop. There were tins of tuna, locally made tomato paste, tinned fruits and vegetables, as well as margarine or butter, powdered milk, coffee, tea, spaghetti, pasta, toothpaste, hand soap, laundry soap, etc. A person could find anything they needed for a price.

We enjoyed filling up a standard shopping cart. When we found what we needed and could afford, we got to the hard part. First, we proceeded through the checkout lane. The cashier totaled up the bill, giving us the receipt. Then we queued at another window to show the receipt to the currency declaration checker. There was always a crowd of fifty people vying for his attention. There was no such thing as an orderly queue. It felt like playing tackle in American football and the declaration checker had the ball. The desk had a stack of forty to fifty currency declaration forms. Sometimes he took one off the top, then one off the bottom, and sometimes out of the middle. More pushy customers tried to find their form and put it in a more advantageous position. However, seeing someone else getting the advantage caused others of us to circumvent them. We put our declarations on top of theirs, back to the order it should have been. When the declaration checker tired of these minor battles, he chose from the bottom instead of the top or vice versa. It took an hour to get MY form in his hands.

He checked how much I owed against how much currency I had listed on the form. After he completed the formalities, he wrote the amount of the purchase on the back of the currency declaration form, and stamped the bill. Then I returned to my goods and paid yet another person. Someone else rechecked the items in my cart, as well as the currency form, before we left the building. There were no refunds.

We found it easier to make our purchases at the Duty Free inside the airport. There was less fuss, and the queues were shorter. They had instant coffee, milk powder, laundry detergent, toothpaste, clothes, electrical appliances, washing machines, televisions, VCRs, and many other things. The only problem with in-the-airport purchases was that the planes arrived in the middle of the night. So, at 2:00 a.m. I wandered around in the Duty Free shop choosing skin cream, dishwashing liquid or purchasing a 50 lb. bag of sugar while the unfortunate person who came to pick me up waited for me to come out. When we got home with the extra goodies, we forgot about any inconvenience.

Love,

L

Dear Harriet,

Now we come to the Battle of the Bugs! I attempted to get rid of the creepy crawlies in the kitchen, but I lost. The ants and roaches invaded, and nothing I used dissuaded them from staying! I might not get rid of all of them, but the more visible ones needed to go. Maybe the answer was to increase the number of geckos. *Hmmm, I wonder how my mother would deal with that?*

I'm reminded of a few earlier times that bugs had been a problem. One day, Janice announced she had gone to Street 15 to buy figs to put in her wonderful fruit compote. Once she got her purchase home, she discovered tiny insects (weevils) in the figs! She confided she had killed them with boiling water and hoped for the best! I don't think anyone noticed.

When I was staying in Juba, a family came from their village location. They were going on leave, so they cleared out the goodies they had saved for that special occasion. Since the raisins might go bad over the long hot season, they brought them to share with others. The cook prepared oatmeal or porridge and put a large handful of raisins in it. They said a prayer of thanks, during which the hostess must have peeked. She managed not to cry out when she saw movement. Upon closer examination, the bugs inhabiting the raisins were evacuating as they heated up from the hot oatmeal. There was a slight delay while they prepared something else for breakfast.

The motto here is: Don't ask what you are eating or look too closely. If you find a weevil, just think of it as added protein.

Which brings me to my final story on this topic for today. In the early days in Juba, we had shipments of food brought in, as there was not much choice in the local market. By the time I arrived in 1983, one of the remaining items in the commissary were boxes of Weetabix. Weetabix is a cereal popular with the British. It is an oval-shaped "brick" of wheat flakes compressed together. You put one or two bricks in your bowl and add milk and sugar. In my experience, they dissolve into mush. And as for flavor, I preferred the box. The ones in Juba contained a growing number of weevils. There was no way to get rid of the weevils except to drown them, but that didn't solve the problem. There was a plentiful supply left, waiting for the unsuspecting newcomer.

Russ made up a commercial about them for a Fun Night at one of our conferences. He advertised Weevilbrix, breakfast of losers! The cereal that increases in protein content the longer it sits on the shelf! I found the script, so let me share it with you.

"Weevilbrix is a seething mass of vitality. It is one of the few breakfast cereals which grows heavier in volume as it awaits road transport to Juba. Weevilbrix provides the adult daily minimum requirement of niacin, thiamine and insect protein. Dozens of people have testified that nothing gets them up from the breakfast table faster than a bowl full of Weevilbrix. Yes, Weevilbrix is like good wine—it really comes to life with age."

Love,

L

———

Dear Harriet,

Our first BIG duty-free purchase was our washing machine. Janice and I planned to acquire one, as we needed to stay on top of the laundry that did not involve hand washing. Washing clothes by hand was one thing, doing sheets and towels was another. We were expecting guests and knew we could never keep up without mechanical help. Off we went with high hopes, our cash, currency declaration forms, and passports.

Our preference was a top loading washer, but they only had front loaders. We found one we could afford ($600) and suffered through the hour of paperwork required to pay for it. We realized there might be a problem when the salesman said, "They will bring it out to your car."

Would it fit in the back of our Suzuki? What if it didn't? I asked, "Could we leave it here until we get a larger vehicle?"

"No. Once you pay for it, you must take it away."

We were relieved when the guys wedged it into the back of the Suzuki. That machine was heavy! Our neighbors helped to get it out once we got home.

Love,

L

———

Dear Harriet,

Our most memorable haboob occurred just as we finished work at 5:00 one afternoon. Janice planned to take our Shilluk colleague James into town and supervise a school certificate exam. But, within three minutes, the world outside turned completely dark, with the wind howling a gale. We looked at each other, wondering what had happened. *Had the electricity gone off?* No, the electricity was still on. But it was dark. *Could it be night?* No, it was only 5:00 in the afternoon; the sun set after 6:00. The wind roared past the windows and the plastic bags were flying by like birds on a speedy migration.

It turned out the haboob began over the irrigation scheme southeast of us and picked up the black cotton soil there. The resulting wall of dust resembled an oil fire and blocked the sun.

While the storm raged, we sat in the living room talking and enjoying the fans. It was the only room without windows, and thus less dusty. The doorbell rang. "Who on earth would visit us in this horrendous storm?" Janice asked. She went to find out, grabbing a scarf to protect her head and face from the dust.

Two welders and a taxi driver stood at the door. The welders had mended our gate once before, and needed to do it again. We had gone to find them a few days before, but no one was there. They were working on a job in town. As they described it, they were "putting together three 'syracles'" (circles) to go in one of the new roundabouts. The storm hit as they neared our house, so they decided to take shelter with us. We sat together drinking Pepsis and visiting as if nothing was happening outside.

When the rain came, the dust mingled with it to create the most amazing marbling effect. Everything looked like Italian marble— the house, walls, cars, trees, everything. The storm stopped after another half an hour, and Janice insisted she had to go supervise the exam. I told her no one would show up for it! And I was right. People just did their best to get home, feeling shaken by the experience.

A few months later, a similar thing happened at 3:00 in the afternoon. This time, the dust was yellow and so thick we didn't see the sun for an hour. It is difficult to explain how disorienting it is to have the world go dark in the middle of the day. I thought, *Is this the Twilight Zone!?* But then I realized, no, it's only Khartoum.

Love,

L

————

Dear Harriet,

We named our house "*Maison maa shaghaal,*" a combination of French (*maison*) and Arabic, meaning "The house that doesn't work." Our house needed more repairs with every passing day. Six repairmen had been in the house in just one day! Four of them reinstalled the air conditioner in Janice's bedroom. This reinstallation entailed rebuilding part of the wall, and at the end, we still had to repaint it ourselves. Despite their best efforts, they put the air conditioner in cockeyed and Janice said she felt drunk if she looked at it too long.

Ibrahim and Mohammed spent their second day at the house working on the large gate behind which we kept the car. I lost the one and only key, so they came to replace the lock on the gate. The next day, the hinges on the gate died. They were too small for the size of the gate, and they broke with frightening regularity.

Then there was the problem with the air vent pipe for the toilet. The builders left a slight angle two feet up from the ground and, more critically, a leak. We tried to seal up the leak several times, to no avail. As soon as the cement hardened, it cracked, and the leak continued. The last plumber that dealt with this handed Janice a small packet of cement to use for the next time it leaked. We began looking for a "good" plumber.

Early one morning, I let out a scream as the toilet blocked up. After trying the normal ways of dealing with this problem, we raised the manhole cover out back. Nothing in my earlier life experiences had prepared me for what was to come. First, we had to spray to kill the significant cockroach population. Then we spent an hour poking and prodding in various drains to find the blockage. At last, I got a pair of pliers and located the source of the blockage: a window handle. Despite the various shortages, this was NOT a normal part of our diet. The landlord was certain one of the Shilluk children had put it there. While that was impossible, he remained unconvinced.

I should explain that Sudanese use water to clean themselves in the bathroom, and so they did not design the septic system to accommodate toilet paper. We had not realized this and were using the normal western procedure. The paper caught on the window handle the workmen left, hence the problem. So, when you see instructions in a hotel in the Middle East that say, "Do not put paper down the toilet," believe them!

Not long after the toilet event, the tap in the kitchen dripped. Within days, it went from a drip to a trickle to a constant flow and we feared it would soon be unstoppable. We turned off the water so we could dismantle the tap. We took the various bits to the Omdurman market to find replacement parts. There was a well-equipped plumbing shop, and as I examined the various taps, a man came over to help me. I soon realized nothing matched the old fittings. To keep this from being a wasted trip, we asked the helpful gentleman if he could recommend a good plumber. He looked embarrassed and explained that he didn't work in the shop, he was just a friend of the owner. "Well," we asked, "does the owner know a good plumber?"

He asked his friend and returned with the verdict, "I know a lot of plumbers, but I don't know any good ones!"

We returned home empty-handed. But having watched my father create solutions, I made washers out of scraps of linoleum and rubber and put the tap back together. It remained drip free for the rest of our stay.

Others handled operations of the house during my Arabic study. Now we had that responsibility, and it was not a small undertaking.

Love,

L

Dear Harriet,

Did you realize the British laid out the center of Khartoum in the shape of the Union Jack? I guess they wanted their presence to be imprinted at the center of life in Khartoum. Sudan switched to driving on the right after independence. Another testimony of British influence is the roundabout. A roundabout manages traffic with no traffic light. Cars entering the roundabout yield to oncoming traffic from their left. If there is an opening to the left, then you can enter the roundabout, and the vehicles to your right need to watch for you. The system works well most of the time. The middle of the roundabout is a round space of varying size. These spaces may be large, other times they are more of a round-a-bump.

During 1989, the government of Sadiq al-Mahdi paid someone to spruce up the roundabouts, as most of them were just masses of brush or overgrown vines. That person, unfortunately, "ate the money," meaning he had taken the money and done nothing. One of the first acts of the Bashir government was to find that person and make him cough up the money. The roundabouts became the talk of the town, and everyone wanted to catch sight of the latest decoration. Soon, we had the fanciest roundabouts in all of Africa!

Traveling along McNimir Road from Nile Avenue, the first roundabout had a middle pillar with "arms" that branched out like a candelabra. In the evening, it reminded us of a speared gecko, so that's what we named it.

The next roundabout on the journey toward Suuq 2 was the "hamburger" roundabout. Atop a pedestal, they placed half a sphere, flat side up. There was a large ball on top of the sphere, with another sphere on top of the ball, again with the flat side up. This configuration reminded us, and others, of hamburger buns, and the ball in the middle was the "burger."

As one continues along McNimir, you come to "the world" roundabout. Four long cement posts supported an enormous globe with a map of the world. That's why we called it "the world."

The curfew-pass office was near the world roundabout. After the coup, the government enforced a curfew from 11:00 p.m. until the call to prayer at 4:30 a.m. If we needed to collect someone from the airport in the middle of the night, officials required us to check in with this office earlier in the day. They took down the license number, the number of passengers, and the place we had to travel. They didn't believe women should drive at that hour, but when I explained there were no men at our compound who could drive, they relented. The police at the checkpoints compared the people in the car with the number on the pass. No extras were allowed.

A few blocks from the world was the *jebana* roundabout. The four coffee pots (*jebana*) were on the medians between the roads entering the roundabout. They painted the coffee pots brown and, on very special occasions, brown liquid (representing coffee) poured out into large white cups with gold stars.

There was a huge metal scroll standing on end in the middle of this roundabout. Most of the foreigners didn't interpret it as a scroll, but gave it the crude title of the "French loo." I've never seen a French toilet, so I can't confirm any resemblances.

The last major roundabout on McNimir changed in appearance as vehicles frequently crashed there. There was a one-way street heading east, so traffic traveled both ways around the roundabout, resulting in nasty accidents. The first thing they put in the roundabout were three gears that locked into each other so nothing would move. Later, they changed it to circles with flashing lights. Each circle had a different color light, and it was distracting. Soon, a crash ended the circuitry and turned the lights off for good. In the end, they put up a simple yellow pillar.

Other roundabouts around the city included the durra stalks in metal, the flame, the Koranic roundabout, the Eiffel tower, and the airplane. The airplane was near our house for a long time. It was an actual plane with flashing lights on it. After some months, they moved the plane closer to the airport and replaced our airplane with a minaret and a fountain.

Speaking of fountains, one of the largest roundabouts was supposed to be a fountain, but they had a hard time keeping the water flowing to it, and it was just a large, round space. One friend drove past this roundabout one evening and saw water spewing into the air. It didn't occur to her that they had fixed the fountain; she thought it was a broken water main.

We appreciated the efforts to beautify the city. It made giving directions a boost in a place that had few street names. The local people resented the government spending so much money on these projects when many had little to eat. The word for roundabout in Arabic is *sinia*, which also means "food tray." So, the Sudanese joked that, "All the trays in Khartoum are full, except the ones for food."

Love,

L

Dear Harriet,

One of the Shilluks who helped us out was James. He had a law degree but had not yet established a law practice. We met him through a German linguist who had been trying to get a handle on Shilluk grammar, but with little success. James had written several Shilluk stories in Arabic as the basis for the analysis. He wanted to write them in Shilluk, but didn't know how. When we met him, he wanted to join forces to solve the problem of written Shilluk.

We asked James how much we should pay him for his time. He thought for a brief time and then gave us amazing advice: "Never pay anyone for working on their own language! They should contribute their time as a way of giving to the community." So, we paid for his transport to our house and back to his or we took him home in our car. Other than cups of tea or bottles of Pepsi, we didn't pay James for the many hours he worked with us. Of course, when we went to Egypt for our vacation, he came with a request, but that is another story.

Pastor Peter and James helped us prepare materials, so we decided it was time to contact the elders in the Shilluk community to get their opinion. We hoped to form a language oversight committee. Each week, we spent many hours visiting various leaders of the Shilluk community. Amos, former Dean of Students at the University of Juba, had moved to Khartoum. He taught in the Extramural Studies Department of the University of Khartoum.

Amos was a teacher and a politician and respected by both southern and northern Sudanese. We soon found our way to his house and spent many hours sitting with him under the large shade tree in his yard. In time, we got acquainted with his wife, Esther, and his five children. They included us as family.

Rev. Samuel was another prominent leader. He pastored the largest of the Shilluk congregations in the Presbyterian Church in greater Khartoum. During the week, he ran one department in the SCC. We spent many hours in his office discussing Shilluk matters and meeting many other important Shilluk people who came to visit. The doorkeeper at SCC got to know us well and immediately admitted us. We attended the Shilluk church service on Sunday evenings and met many of the Protestant leaders and the youth, who became leaders.

Our strategy during the week was to go to an office where a Shilluk elder worked, introduce ourselves, and explain what we were trying to do with the writing. Most people agreed Shilluk was very difficult to read. Early missionaries had set up schools using Shilluk language materials for the first three years of primary school. Those were very simple readers, and there were no other books between those and the New Testament. At one point, it was a capital offense to own books in local languages! Now they did not even try to read anything in Shilluk. They acknowledged there was a problem and were glad someone was interested in fixing it. Without exception, they loved their language and believed it was key to protecting their culture and heritage.

We drank sweet tea by the gallon as we got to know our host. Then we inquired if there were other Shilluks that we should meet. Sometimes those people "just happened" to drop by the office and we discussed our plan with several people at once. Most of the time, though, we had to tackle the elders one by one.

One of our most interesting visits was to Sabino, a prominent Catholic leader. The northern Shilluks were Catholic, or they were Presbyterian if from the southern part of Upper Nile Province. Sabino was the director of the Catholic Relief agency. I met him because Sister Theresa sent a letter to me through Sabino's office. She addressed the letter to "Leoma Nyacyängjwøk" and included my phone number. He knew every Shilluk in town except this one. Nyacyängjwøk is my Shilluk name and means "born on Sunday." He wanted to find out who this was, so he contacted me to say he had a letter for me, and would I come by his office to collect it? When a white woman showed up, he wondered what was going on. I explained I had been working on Shilluk for six years and was trying to improve the writing system. I learned later that when he heard I had spent that much time studying his language, he decided I deserved to have a hearing. So, he arranged the first Shilluk Language Oversight Committee meeting in his office on December 1, 1989. All those cups of tea and hours of visiting paid off as a dozen elders turned up for that first meeting.

At our insistence, the committee should represent both dialect areas and all religious preferences. We never got women on the committee, but they included both dialects in any decisions. On that first day, they agreed on the alphabet and decided to meet regularly. One of the first changes they insisted on was the name of the language. Instead of Shilluk, which they consider an Arabic distortion of their real name, they wanted to use Cøllø. The correct pronunciation is "chaw–law." Janice and I felt that the literacy work was off and running.

Love,

L

Dear Harriet,

By September 8, the government implemented price controls. Since the set price was below cost, merchants closed up their shops rather than lose money. We had shortages of gasoline, sugar, flour, bread, and meat. Life is challenging, but I know I'm where I'm supposed to be.

Sundays are full days. We head over to the American Club to swim, have lunch, and relax. At 4:30 we might visit with Amos, a Shilluk friend, and his family. Then we attend the Shilluk church service at 6:00. When it is over, we drop into the English service before heading home.

During the Christmas season, an American family invited us to a carol sing. Patty made mountains of cookies and a surprise birthday cake! Given that sugar and white flour are almost impossible to find, it was amazing and delightful.

The government is paranoid about people sending foreign currency in or out of the country by mail, so they check everything, even air forms. They hanged one man in December 1989 for dealing on the black market and another for possession of opium. This government doesn't fool around. The US threatened to break diplomatic relations, and we wait to see what that might mean for us.

People are discouraged and feel hopeless. If I can offer progress in literacy, it may be an encouragement to a few. Most importantly, though, is the value of people's prayers for this country and for me because I'm here. This place needs mega prayers. I feel well and safe. I'd find it more comfortable to be home, but I am accomplishing something here, even against the odds.

Love,

L

Dear Harriet,

James had started two trial classes while we were away, one in Hai Jusef and the other in North Khartoum. The Hai Jusef class had fifteen students, some of whom were on the committee. The older men liked to argue with James, as that is their duty. They commended him for teaching well, agreeing that the book was 75 percent correct, which I took as high praise. The North Khartoum class had thirty students, and when James wanted to stop at 6:00 after teaching for two hours, they demanded he continue for another hour.

James, in the striped shirt, teaching a lesson

I got certificates ready for those completing the various classes and completed two storybooks and the alphabet book. I also prepared my PhD thesis for typesetting in Nairobi, sending twenty-one pages of corrections.

One evening, we drove to Duty Free to see what was available. We arrived at 5:30 instead of 5:00 and found the place packed with people. We chose what turned out to be $34 worth of food items such as sandwich spread, jam, and ketchup. They were double that price in the shops if you could find them. We waited in a queue for one and a half hours to pay for it. I had a $50 traveler's cheque. They didn't give any change, so we had to choose $16 worth of things to buy. That meant an hour's wait to get them recorded. Finally, the lady had pity on me and wrote the rest of my purchases (mayonnaise, asparagus, and a tin of candy) on the original bill. I retrieved my currency declaration form and headed for the door. Fifteen minutes later, they finished checking my purchases against my bill. We got away at 7:15. By then, we both needed a drink, especially as the air conditioning wasn't working. We dropped by to visit friends and had a glass of water and a cup of tea.

For supper, we had an ear of corn. My! We were excited as that's the first corn I have seen in a long time. When I leave Sudan, I will become a "Cucumber-Free Zone." Cucumbers are ubiquitous, and I was tired of them after the first week!

Prices have gone up yet again, and I don't know how the Sudanese are managing. A sack of grain is $90, and the average income for a family is only $60 per month. An extra-large box of laundry soap is $37. Toothpaste is unobtainable.

Love,

L

Dear Harriet,

Back on the home front, the government took a census. I participated in one in the US while in college. It involved answering a page of questions and mailing it back. Well, that is NOT how Sudan conducts a census.

First, many Sudanese cannot read or write. Second, the internal postal system is not reliable. Third, with a civil war going on in much of the country, there is no way to get forms to them. Fourth, certain groups dislike revealing how many children they have, as the spirits might decide you are bragging and kill a few to pay you back for your pride. Also, they believe the taxes will increase based on the number of children you have. So, the fewer you report, the better. As you can see, getting accurate information is a challenge.

On the appointed day, the government announced everyone had to stay at home. No one should leave their house until after 4:00 p.m. Our landlord came over ahead of time to make sure we understood these rules. We busied ourselves, knowing that we would not have company or interruptions. We wondered how well we could communicate with the census taker? In the end, we didn't have to worry. Our landlord's son, Aiman, took the census in our neighborhood.

He came to the door with his stack of papers and a pen and announced that he would take the details of our household. First, he had to see everyone in the house. Of course, he knew there were only the two of us, since Peter and his family had moved out a couple of months before. Then he wanted our names, our fathers' names, and our paternal grandfathers' names. I explained my father's name was J.T., but we used surnames and mine was Gilley. Likewise, my grandfather's name was L.H., but his surname was also Gilley. As far back as I could go, our family name was Gilley. This amazed Aiman, and his remark enlightened me. "I've heard of naming systems like that, but I wasn't sure! How do you know how you are related?"

By explanation, I should say that in the Sudanese system, they give each person a name when they are born. Their second name is their father's first name. His third name is his grandfather's first name. So, since Aiman's father was Abdul and let's assume his grandfather's name was Muhammed, then Aiman's full name would be Aiman Abdul Muhammed. We found understanding relationships confusing in that system, just as they found ours mystifying.

Other questions included our religion, where we came from, and whether we owned a car. The harmless survey finished in half an hour. I wondered if getting the same information in other homes was as easy as it had been in ours. About 4:00 p.m., we noticed the local population on the move, visiting each other. The census was over.

Love,

L

Chapter 3:
1990

Dear Harriet,

It is January 1, 1990. Janice and I have been in Khartoum for almost a year! For the first time, we have a ration card that allows us to buy basic commodities when they are available. We also have a fuel ration card, although the title of the car is still not in our names. We've bought two new tires. We must purchase things when we can, even if we don't need them. We have the Suzuki Jeep, the house, and access to several Shilluks. The newly formed Shilluk Language Oversight Committee has approved the alphabet. We know how to get around the city. Janice spent several weeks with her family over the Christmas holidays. I had dreaded being alone, but God took up the slack.

After Janice returned, John and Pam, our literacy consultants, came to visit for a couple of weeks. We worked together, planning the best way to run a literacy program in Khartoum. They joined us at the committee meeting to reinforce my ideas. Some of my suggestions ran counter to the basic assumptions Shilluks had regarding their language. I wanted the spelling decisions made so that Janice could write the English to Shilluk transition book. Many people were eager to take classes.

Love,

L

Dear Harriet,

The Cøllø Language Oversight Committee met each Friday at 10:30. Rev. Samuel hosted the meetings at the SCC since people were off work and free to come. Ten to twelve men came to discuss the technical issues of their language. We prepared examples to illustrate the various problems and then offered one or more solutions. Amos served as the chairman of the committee and so we briefed him before each meeting.

The meetings continued for an hour and a half, but sometimes longer. The members enjoyed arguing with each other, so they went on and on.

Once everyone arrived, Janice and I presented the topic of the day. We learned that in Cøllø society, each person needed to have his or her say. Most of the discussion was in English, but sometimes in Cøllø or Arabic. At an unexpected point, the chairman said, "Now that has been decided, we will move on to the next topic."

The problem was, I didn't know what they had decided, and I was taking the notes of the meetings. I asked, "What was the decision?"

Usually the answer was, "We agreed with your suggestion." It took close observation to discover what signaled the end of the discussion. Each person spoke their mind to get the issue thrashed out. The discussion continued until they agreed. When the last two speakers said the same thing, those statements summarized the consensus.

Many of the decisions involved issues in the grammar of Cøllø. When referring to non-Arabic languages, Sudanese use the word *rotaan* (gibberish). The men excitedly realized their language is a REAL language, like Arabic and English, because it has a grammar!

After several months of meeting, they accepted most of my suggestions and gave us the go-ahead to produce an English to Cøllø transition book. We used these books to teach those who read English to understand the new Cøllø writing system.

Love,

L

Dear Harriet,

We decided to print five hundred copies of the transition book.

Janice was the literacy expert, but none of us living in Khartoum had ever made a book. We printed our master copies at 2:00 a.m. because of the power shortages. Next, Janice pasted on the pictures. Then we photocopied the masters and used Wite-Out to cover the extraneous black lines.

When we left Juba, the administration transported the equipment used in the literacy center in Maridi to Khartoum. We used that to make the books. There was an electronic stencil cutter and boxes of stencils. We put our master on one side of a drum and the stencil next to it. An electronic pen moved across the stencil, duplicating the pattern of words or pictures from the master, cutting the images into the stencil. It is primitive, and we felt we were working in the Dark Ages. At least we didn't have to type and draw the images by hand!

Once we made the stencil, we put the stencil on an old spirit duplicator. I think the original meaning of "spirit" refers to the kind of ink. Ours had a life of its own, but more of that soon.

Next, we needed paper. There were no employees or staff from our office available to buy it. That shouldn't have been a problem, but we didn't know that where they sold paper and ink was a "men only" section. When we turned up one morning to buy paper and ink, we wondered why we were hearing remarks, and getting not a few funny looks.

We found paper. The cheapest was $11 for 480 sheets (one ream). Once we got the ten reams back to the office, we groaned. In each package, there were at least two widths, three to four lengths, and two to three weights of paper. Some of the paper came with huge creases that wouldn't come out. But that was what we could afford, so we made the best of it. We purchased two tubes of ink and borrowed another one and a half tubes to finish the run of books.

Our next challenge involved getting to the office when there was electricity. The old generator needed lots of tender loving care, and only certain people should start it. We were NOT on that list, though we cranked it up a few times. The duplicator sat in the hottest room in the entire building, a tiny room with few windows. Outside the long wall was the unshaded, oven-like verandah. When power and water were both available, we turned on the closest air cooler and put a fan in our small window to attract the cooler air. I guess it helped.

We loaded the duplicator with ink, wrapped the stencil around the drum, and placed the paper as neatly as we could on the input tray. The duplicator operated with a hand crank, and we should have used that. But since it could function with electricity (and it was hot and humid), we opted to use that. It started at a sensible speed, picking up one sheet, pulling it past the master on the drum and pushing it out the far side into the paper tray. However, twenty-five to fifty sheets into our run of five hundred, it sped up. We hadn't noticed the speed regulator knob had moved to a faster position as the machine vibrated. The pace got faster and faster until it picked up ten sheets of paper at once and shoved them through the machine. Once they reached the far side, they shot in all directions. Janice and I grabbed for them as they wheeled and flew around the room. When we counted the readable copies produced, we had to run more because so many had caught only half the stencil or none. Many pages got smeared and were unreadable.

When we completed one side, the ink had to dry, and then, we ran the back side. The same process happened time after time. We thought the electricity had varied, and it was well into the job before we discovered the knob causing the changes in speed. We should have known more about our equipment before we started and had someone handy to help. In the end, we eked out two hundred copies and felt exhausted after weeks of work. There was LOTS of scrap paper and we wondered if this effort would ever pay off.

We had purchased sheets of yellow poster paper and spent hours cutting it up for the book covers. We printed one side with the title and a picture. The last part of the process involved collating the 120 pages, and then, using a long arm stapler, stapling the pages together. It was a labor of love. No one could pay me enough to go through that much misery.

Happily, I can report James used the book and proved to be an excellent teacher. His first class had fourteen students. He taught while we sat in the back, observed, and answered questions. Several of the participants became teachers and worked long term with the literacy project. We went on vacation and James started another three classes with sixty-three people. It was indeed an encouraging start.

Love,

L

Dear Harriet,

We had arrived in Khartoum on February 12, and after a year, it was time to celebrate. Janice and I headed to the Friendship Palace Hotel for a chocolate moo, a chocolate ice cream with whipped cream in a fancy dish. It was Janice's mother's birthday, so she tried to phone her. That was always a procedure. We first booked the call with the Sudanese international operator, who then connected to their counterpart in the other country (US or UK). Once they spoke, we hoped to get through to the person's phone. We had to say in advance how many minutes we wanted to talk, and at the end of that time, we got cut off, ready or not. Janice never reached her mom that day.

We reminisced about the past year and the challenges we had faced.

With the currency restrictions, paying rent proved challenging. Landlords wanted payment in US dollars. But we couldn't keep USD even in a bank. When we withdrew it, we got Sudanese pounds. We found other ways to make our payments. For example, I sent a check to my parents for three months' rent. They deposited it in my account. Then a bank in Switzerland charged my bank and put it into the landlord's account. It was illegal to make this transaction in the country.

Another edict proclaimed all shops should have white walls and green doors. Given there are very few street names, directions for finding someone's house depended on the color of walls, shops, and gates. If every shop had white walls with green doors, giving clear directions would be impossible. In fact, we gave someone directions to a location that involved a dark-red brick building. She couldn't find it because they had painted it white. The photographer at our house spent time and effort painting the doors to his shop a bright variety of colors: red, blue, yellow, green. Now he had to cover that with green. We suspected someone connected to power acquired an excessive amount of white and green paint they wanted to sell.

How many people have you seen in the back of a Toyota pickup? Our answer one day was twenty, with four more in the cab. Public buses are erratic and overcrowded, so if a pickup is going their way, men jump on. As people got off the truck, we saw others sitting down besides the seventeen Janice counted who were standing.

Joe and Marianne came to Khartoum from Washington state for six months to do fix-it jobs. We needed a good bit of fixing at our place.

We heard the war in the south cost the government $2.5 million a day. As a result, there were serious shortages. It cost us $80/week for food and necessities. Most Sudanese only make the equivalent of $50/month. The exchange rate didn't change for more than a year, but inflation was running at 10 percent per month.

A friend of ours purchased a car and ended up visiting 108 desks in various ministries over three days to complete the process. He still didn't have the license plates.

Yes, it had been a challenging year, but we survived to tell about it. And the chocolate moo was delicious.

Love,

L

Dear Harriet,

Jo lived in a third-floor apartment with an excellent view into her neighbor's courtyard. They were not very devout Muslims as they never fasted during Ramadan, at least not in their home. Outside, they didn't eat or drink, but inside they did both. This brings me to the other side of Ramadan: the people who don't fast.

Janice, Jo, and I stopped off once again for a cool fruit drink at the Friendship Palace Hotel. Their juice was delicious. We sat outside on the patio for a long time before we realized it was Ramadan, and no one would serve us in public. So, we moved inside to the restaurant and found it was full. If someone is going to cheat during this month, they go to a part of town where no one knows them. Then, in the privacy of a hotel, they eat, drink, and smoke anonymously. Since everyone else is doing the same thing, they are safe from accusation or embarrassment.

One Christian Sudanese told me how he got food during Ramadan. He and non-religious Muslims wanted to eat, but shops had to be locked. The proprietor might sit outside, and if you slipped money to him, he would unlock the door. Once inside, he shut and locked it again. Inside, the cook served food. The customers devoured it and then tapped on the door. This alerted the owner to let them out. As far as I know, only men patronized these places.

I went to the Meridien Hotel restaurant during Ramadan for lunch. Since travelers do not have to fast, hotels could offer meals when other places had to stay closed. It was risky, as the morality police might come in with whips. If they found Muslims eating, they began whipping them. I never saw this happen, but several people reported it had occurred.

If you are starving and thirsty, getting tangled up in traffic will try your patience more than usual. Traffic jams were a significant part of life during Ramadan. Everyone was in a grumpy mood from lack of sleep, food, and drink. They just wanted to reach their work, carry out what had to be done, and go home to rest. Drivers became short-tempered and tried to push into nonexistent spaces ahead of the other cars. I got caught in a jam on a wide two-lane road with eight lanes of cars going in one direction. One oncoming lane skirted around the electrical poles since there was no space left on the road. At the intersection, passengers jumped from pickup trucks to direct the traffic, as no one was moving anywhere.

We decided it was best not to drive in the hour before *fatuur*. Just wait a few minutes. After the call to prayer, the roads are empty.

Love,

L

Dear Harriet,

We decided it was spring when temperatures rose to 105°-110°F in the day but cooled down to 80°F at night. Temperatures in our house remained 80°-95°F. It is the season for the flowers to fade and die. In 1990, spring lasted five days and then temperatures inside rose to 101°F. At this point in the year, we did a lot of furniture moving. We moved chairs and a table out into the garden in the afternoon to enjoy the coolness. About 9:30, we returned the furniture inside and brought out our mattresses and mosquito nets and *angareebs*. The house is too hot to sleep inside without using the air conditioners, and if the power goes out, they are no use anyway. By 2:00 a.m., I needed a blanket. At 6:00, the sun rose and the flies came out, so we moved back inside. It is haboob season, so dust is a constant wherever you are.

In March 1990, we welcomed a visitor from England for a week. Her visit provided a great excuse to show her the sights and see them ourselves. We had enjoyed a nice boat cruise on the Nile to celebrate someone's birthday, so we took our visitor on a similar outing. As we inquired about prices, they seemed high. One advertisement in the Acropole Hotel suggested a more economical solution. So, we signed up and on the agreed day, headed to the shores of the Blue Nile. We drove through fields of soybeans and vegetables to a small grass shed. Our captain led us along a narrow path down a steep bank to the river. The rich black soil deposited each year by the Nile floods was now a dry, gray dust that rose in clouds around our feet.

Once we reached the river, we were dismayed to find a pontoon boat with no roof. They spread the canvases from two patio umbrellas over the metal frame where the roof should have been. Those umbrellas provided us five square feet of shade to huddle under to escape the fiery rays of the midday sun. We had asked if there was a toilet available during this trip. They assured us this would not be a problem. Likewise, we asked if they provided refreshments, and again, they assured they would provide everything. It was the middle of Ramadan, so the captain and everyone else were fasting. No one could eat or drink all day, so we felt we couldn't either, even if it had been available. We spent two hours nestled in our little patch of shade with not a sip of water. At least I didn't need to use the nonexistent toilet. We felt dried up and shriveled by the time our trip ended. Despite the difficulties, we saw wonderful birds and examined weaverbird nests up close. My best photos of Sudanese birds came from that trip. The rhythm of the river helped us relax as we rocked along, like Tom Sawyer on a raft. It was a memorable experience for us.

Our visitor, Joy, had fair skin and the slightest exposure to the sun left her a bright shade of pink. So, it was a relief to get to shore, climb the bank, and settle into our Suzuki. We each drank a gallon of water once we got to the house. As we sat in our sitting room, melting in the early March heat wave, I told our visitor, "It will be this temperature again later in the year; only then it will be getting cooler." In other words, it was not yet as hot as it would be in a few months. She didn't return to check.

In the middle of Joy's stay, Janice suggested she reconfirm her flight back to England. Her travel agent had said it was unnecessary, as she had a confirmed booking. Janice persisted, since Joy needed to be at work on Monday morning. Joy conceded and off they headed to town. The agent at Air France looked at the ticket and exclaimed, "That flight hasn't existed for over six months!" London may have confirmed it, but it didn't exist in Khartoum. They agreed Joy had to leave two days early to be back in England to get to work. She came back to our house and started packing.

Love,

L

Dear Harriet,

After Joy's abrupt departure, we thought about what we had endured the previous summer. Remembering the long power cuts in that stifling house motivated us to move. Besides, only a handful of Cøllø visitors came during the entire year. Many Cøllø lived in Hai Jusef, but to travel by public transport to Fitihab took much of the day. Then they needed to get home again. So, we decided we should live as close to the center of Khartoum as possible. We started house hunting.

Every place seemed hotter than the one before. It was a discouraging prospect until one day we ran into Alistair. He had rented a house in Mogran for less than half of what we were paying. He ran a recording studio in one of the outside buildings. The problem was, he didn't have a residence permit and thus could not legally rent a house. One of his employees lived in the garage and they used the storeroom as a studio. A university student had lived in the house but could not stay. He needed someone with legal status to live there. It sounded odd, but we agreed to have a look.

The location was half a mile from the confluence of the Blue and White Niles, near the Hilton Hotel. The Mogran community elected a sheik to oversee the needs of each household. In the middle of the neighborhood was a large garden that cooled the air. The yard was cement, so there was no grass to worry about. There were plenty of trees and large verandahs on three sides of the house. Inside were two bedrooms, a sitting room, bathroom, and kitchen. It was small, simple, centrally located, and best of all, it was CHEAP! We agreed to take it on the spot.

When we agreed to rent the house, we didn't know it was on a special electricity line. Once we moved, we had electricity twenty-four hours a day, seven days a week, to the envy of our friends.

The only things we needed to do before we moved were: (1) break the bad news to our landlord, Abdul, (2) move our things to the new location, and (3) reclaim our air cooler from the landlord's rented house. We found the new house at the beginning of May, just as our lease ended. Abdul was not happy that we failed to give him advance notice, because he had a lease as well. In the end, we agreed to pay an extra month's rent in compensation. Once we sorted that out, we asked our Nuer neighbor to use their truck. We paid for fuel and a bit extra, but we realized we had not offered enough in compensation, because toward the end of the move, the truck became "unavailable." On our last day, as we packed the last loads into the Suzuki, we moved the cats.

Even though both cats had male names, they were females. We named them after the two political leaders that were in control of the north and the south. We used to joke that this was our contribution to the peace agreement. The Cølløs laughed at our choice of names, but we got the idea from them. As I understand it, they name animals and people after situations. They used to tell me not to say the names too loudly or I might be arrested. I don't think anyone ever noticed.

Anyway, Sadiq hated cars and moving. She never enjoyed having her world disrupted. However, on the advice of a colleague, we put her in a pillowcase and a helpful Sudanese held her all the way to the new house. We deposited her in Janice's room since it was the easiest to close up. She took up residence behind a mattress and didn't leave that room for three days.

Garang took more convincing. She disappeared the whole day we were moving. She never liked strangers in our house. We looked and looked for her. *Would we have to leave her behind?* But, at the end of our last pickup, there she was, appearing from thin air. I petted her and picked her up. She accepted this, and I slipped her into a pillowcase. Well, let me tell you, the trip to Mogran was not a happy one for anyone in that car. We kept the windows up to keep her from jumping out and there wasn't enough left of the pillowcase to bother with when it was over. We deposited her in the same room with her sister and went to tend to our scratches.

Sadiq on the verandah

Love,

L

Dear Harriet,

The plan of most Sudanese houses starts with two rooms built off-center of each other. In the diagram below, the solid lines show the original rooms. One room served as the parents' bedroom and the other as the children's bedroom. The wife used the children's room to receive her visitors. The husband received his guests outside the parents' bedroom. A kitchen was located a short distance from the two main rooms in a separate and less well-constructed building. The long-drop toilet was separate from the rest of the house. As soon as they can afford it, the family puts a roof over the path between the two rooms and encloses the verandahs on both sides. The thin line shows the verandahs. The outer line is the wall around the compound.

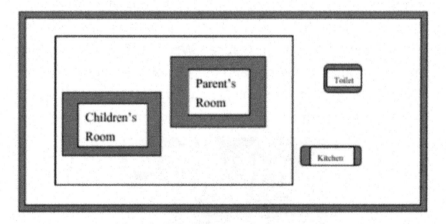

How most Sudanese homes are designed

After this addition, there were two doorways to the outside, one in the front and one in the back. This arrangement provided ventilation and a place for visitors to enter (in the front). The hostess brought food and drink to guests from the kitchen (in the back). They added other rooms as needed.

Our new house started out on this plan but now included the kitchen, bathroom, and servant's quarters under one roof. The landlady had enclosed an outside verandah to serve as our main sitting room. Doric columns supported the verandah, and three were prominent features of our living room. The window into the bedroom had security grating along with two sets of shutters, one set with glass, and one set with wooden slats. They left these extras from when it served as an outside window. The second bedroom was smaller than the first, and the windows only had solid wooden shutters and security grating. Even the door was smaller. We decided this room had been the servant's quarters in an earlier time. Janice's wardrobe barely went through the door, and we had to take the door off the kitchen to get the refrigerator inside. The kitchen and Janice's bedroom doors were about the same size.

Because it had been an outside porch, tiles of various colors and styles covered the floor in the living room. They had tiled over the drains, but the dip was still there. Many tiles were broken or loose and rattled as you walked across them. Later, we discovered there was only a dirt base on the floor with tiles laid on top.

A couple of sheets of plywood covered in tar paper formed the roof. The ceiling displayed a charming array of long nails pounded through the plywood. The thin covering of tar paper attempted to protect the living room from rain. We added a ceiling to cover up the protruding nails and to give more insulation from the heat of the sun. That was the hottest room in the house, as it had the thinnest and the lowest ceiling.

The landlady had moved to Australia but left her things in the unoccupied middle rooms of the house. Her plan was to rent either side, and if she returned to stay in Sudan, she expected to live in the middle section. That idea never came to be.

This time, we called on some Sudanese friends to paint the house for us. We limited our help to interfering and telling them not to water down the paint and fussing because they splashed paint on the tiles of the floor. The windows got a healthy dose of paint as well, but since they were frosted glass, it didn't matter so much.

The best part of the house was the kitchen. It came with light-blue metal cupboards, two sets mounted on a wall and two free standing ones with a Formica countertop. There was also an old shallow stone sink with a wooden drainboard attached. We just added a fridge, my little oven, and a table. We cooked up a storm.

The eight-foot-deep verandah served as a great place to receive visitors until the afternoon. It faced west, so as the sun set, it became more difficult to find a shaded place to sit. Surrounding the compound were lovely, tall eucalyptus and neem trees, which protected us from the worst of the heat.

The front of the Mogran house (Credit: Kathy Smith)

The side of the Mogran house (Credit: Kathy Smith)

Our new house had two outbuildings; one served as an office for the recording work. The other provided housing for a guard. It also had a toilet and shower. We invited a new friend, Peter M, to come to live there as his brother didn't have room for him anymore. He was grateful for a place to live, and we came to value his presence more and more each day.

Love,

L

Dear Harriet,

In planning to move to our new house in Mogran, we needed to buy a refrigerator. That meant another trip to Duty Free! The fridge wasn't all that big, but cost $800. But life without a fridge in 100°F heat isn't worth the effort. Even though our new place had fewer power cuts, it came with a small generator. We never needed it.

We hired a Cøllø friend to work on the wiring in the house. Electricity in Khartoum was a new adventure for me. I had never seen fuse wire, only fuses. But, in 1990, fuse wire was common, or rather should have been. Our main fuse box had a nail in it instead of fuse wire. I guess they got tired of it breaking when the voltage was too high.

We found a 240-volt light switch IN the shower. Our friend moved it outside the bathroom door. He changed the incandescent light fixtures to fluorescent ones. The one plug anywhere near the fridge was in the next room. So, he added a new one in the kitchen. He also added an outlet for the washing machine on the back verandah.

After being in our new home for ten days, we had only experienced one 20-second power cut. The rest of Khartoum was still having twelve to eighteen hours of power cuts. We learned many influential people owned family homes in Mogran, and they have influence. We heard that access to the switches to turn off the power to Mogran are locked and only a few employees have the keys. So, if the electricity is off, there is a problem. It is not because they don't have enough for everyone.

The new house was half the size of the Fitihab one. There were no built-in closets, so we purchased free-standing wardrobes. A tiny air cooler was already above the main entrance to the sitting room. Once we got both air coolers working, we slept inside at night. Outside is okay, but when a dust storm comes, you get covered with grit and the wind keeps you awake. With better sleep, I can cope with the heat, humidity, and work.

The Cølløs say, "The sun is hungry." That means "Boy, it is boiling hot!" With regular power and water, we lived a more "normal" lifestyle since we stayed cool and our refrigerator kept cold! What a blessing.

Love,

L

Dear Harriet,

Having settled in our new home, we wanted to invite people to visit. How should we give them directions? Peter M sorted us out on that. He asked, "Have you seen the tire at the end of the road?"

"No," but we investigated. Sure enough, there was a tire standing upright, but half buried in the ground.

"Tell people to turn on the road with the tire."

Believe it or not, those directions were clear, and no one had trouble locating us. Even after workers removed the tire during some roadwork, we could still say, "Do you remember the tire? That's where you turn." It worked.

Our growing collection of furniture fit perfectly in the house. The first week, we received more Cøllø visitors than in the entire year we had spent in Fitihab. Our new friends came to see where we were living. They entered our gate, walked up on the verandah, and then entered our large front door into the sitting room. Invariably they dropped into a chair, looked around at the tiny room and said, "This is a nice house. This is a good house for you." They were at home and we knew we had found the right home for everyone to feel comfortable.

Our neighborhood had a small grocery store, a tailor, and a tire repair shop. The tailor produced an amazing variety of clothing. He made dresses for women and children, fancy or plain, but always colorful. I never saw his machine, but he knew how to use it. Women in the area appreciated his services, and he made a reasonable living.

The other shop repaired flat tires. The equipment in this tiny cubicle included a good-sized tub of water (to find the leak in the inner tube), a pressurized air pump, and a crowbar for breaking the tire off the wheel. They also had a mounting machine to get the tire onto the wheel and a good supply of tire glue to fix the holes. Whenever my tire was leaking air, I stopped in to add more. They didn't charge for that service. I tried to pay them, but they never accepted the money. Most hoses had no air pressure gauge and wouldn't work with the metal tip in the tire's stem. So, they pulled out the metal tip and filled the tire by guesswork until it was fuller than it needed to be. Then they took the hose off and stuck the metal tip back in the stem. They then tested the pressure and let out the excess air. Maybe it was easier to do that than find the money to put the proper end on their air hose.

Whenever I drove up with a flat tire, they leapt up from their chairs and set to fixing it. They threw the tire onto the ground, and then one man jumped on it while the other used the crowbar to break it loose from the wheel. Once it was free, they jerked out the inner tube and put air into it. They found the leak and then lickety-split, patched up the hole. Next, they searched to find a nail and pull it out with a handy pair of pliers. Then they threw the inner tube back inside the tire and put it back onto the rim with a loud POP. The entire process took ten minutes and cost a dollar.

Once I had a flat when the shop was closed. Peter M walked to the main road with the tire to get it repaired in town, and in a bit, a bus stopped for him. They didn't charge him to ride into town. When I asked him about it, he said, "Well, they realize one day they may have a problem and need help. Today, they helped me." It's part of life in a community.

Love,

L

Dear Harriet,

Life in our little "village" started before the sun rose. Soon after the call to prayer, about 4:30 a.m., the bean sellers began washing out their large round bean pots to prepare for the new batch of *fuul*. The bean pots were like an industrial-sized metal balloon on the bottom and they had a small mouth at the top. They put the Egyptian beans and water in together, then placed the pot over a charcoal fire. Once the beans heated up, they put a large rock on top to "keep the lid on." It took several hours, so an early start was necessary to be ready to serve the *fuul* for breakfast by 9:00 a.m.

When the beans were ready, the customers materialized. They each received a small, shallow metal bowl filled with one scoop of beans and broth. The customer chose more options: sesame seed oil, chopped onions, falafel (fried chickpea balls), cumin, hot peppers, feta cheese, salt, and lime. Everything tastes better with a squeeze of *leemun* (lime). Two long, thin loaves of freshly baked bread served as utensils to eat the beans. Sudanese eat using their right hand.

Customers squatted on their heels or sat on a low stool. If several people ordered together, they got a larger, shared dish. Sharing food is an important statement of friendship. Enemies will not eat together. The meal ended with a soda and/or a cup of strong, steaming hot, sweet tea.

A customer who couldn't afford to pay for the meal ($.30) ordered the cheap alternative—just the bean juice poured over broken pieces of bread. This provided nourishment from the juice and bread to fill the stomach. I noticed an increased popularity for this as times got harder and salaries didn't go far enough.

Some of the hardest working members of the community scene were the tea ladies. Most of them lived in the displaced areas on the outskirts of the city. However, communities like ours provided an opportunity. Each morning, they brought their charcoal stoves, tea glasses, and tins of coffee and tea and set up shop. If the household near their stand was amenable, they would leave their things in the compound. I noticed Peter M had agreed to such an arrangement for one of the tea ladies outside our house.

The tea ladies always wore *tobes*. They draped this long colorful cloth over their dress to be modest and obedient to the Islamic dress code. The refreshment stand was a simple affair made of a wooden crate or small table. The space was only one foot square. On the table they had tins containing coffee beans, tea leaves, crushed ginger, a mix of cinnamon, cloves, and cardamom, and a large one for sugar. They kept a jerry can of water handy for the drinks and later for washing the cups and spoons. There was a small plastic basin for dish washing. Soap did not figure into the washing regime.

Several customers are enjoying a hot drink from our local tea lady

After setting up, they lit a few pieces of charcoal and soon the smoldering coals heated the water in a tin teapot. Several low metal and string *banbars* or footstools provided seating for the lady and her customers. Tea is such an intrinsic part of waking up and getting through the day, and customers appeared quickly. The seller put a small juice glass on the table and asked how much sugar the customer wanted. Most people prefer two to five heaping teaspoons! Then she put the tea leaves in a strainer and poured hot water over them into the glass. A quick stir, and the drink was ready. She might add spices; cinnamon, cloves, and cardamom were favorites and are delicious.

Coffee took longer. The process required roasting the beans and crushing them with spices using a mortar and pestle. They use either cardamom or ginger and then put the spiced grounds in a *jebana* or clay coffee pot. The *jebana* is round on the bottom with a narrow neck and a rounded handle for pouring. They stuff bits of dried grass into the mouth of the *jebana* to act as a strainer so the grounds don't come out at once. They then pour the strong mixture into a demitasse-sized cup with no handle.

In the old days, before sugar was available, the Sudanese used dates to sweeten their coffee. Nowadays, sugar is more common. The grounds, sugar, and spice fill half of the cup. The remaining sips likely have the caffeine of a large cup of "normal" coffee. The price covers the whole *jebana*, three "cups" of coffee.

A *jebana* for coffee, and used as a symbol of the Sudan

After coming early in the morning, these ladies did not return home until 8:00 p.m. They often left young children in the care of older ones. If a baby became sick or injured during the day, the mother would not know until she arrived home in the evening. Then she needed to prepare a meal for her family and deal with any other issues that arose. Children didn't get the attention they should have, but selling tea was one of the few legal jobs poor, uneducated women could do.

Large Pepsi trucks rumbled along the streets, and we heard the clank of cases of full bottles replacing empty ones throughout the day. At the end of the street, there was a gas bottle store. They collected empty gas bottles for the truck bringing full ones. A new bottle cost $5. There were several kinds, and each one had a different regulator. We kept the blue and the orange, but never got the green ones.

Throughout the day, various mobile salesmen came by on their donkeys. The milkman knocked on the gates of his regular customers. Sometimes we heard *akyaas*! (bags) from a man on donkey-back, selling sisal sacks that once held grain. At other times, the caller offered charcoal or brooms. The jingle of a tambourine alerted us to the shoeshine boy.

The milkman on his donkey (Credit: Kathy Smith)

Around 1:00 p.m., things got quiet. The call to prayer from the mosque and later the rowdy boys playing in the street were the only sounds. Their parents had likely sent them out of the house so the adults could get a little sleep. Most people reached home from work around 2:00 p.m. and rested before eating lunch. In the afternoons, a toy horn signaled someone selling candy. Through the afternoon, the sun blazed, and if I had to walk somewhere between 2:00 and 4:00, I felt as if I were alone on the planet. A few men near the shops sitting in the shade of an awning or tree wondered what was so urgent that I had to be out at that hour. I wondered about that too.

By 4:30, life began again. A block away from the house was a large *medaan*, or square, for the local football (soccer) matches. The Sudanese love soccer. Simon, Peter M's half-brother, played on the local team and was so talented that he made third string on the national team. His goal in life is to be another Pele. The Mogran soccer ball had seen better days, the goal no longer had a net, and the field was marked off with chalk. An enthusiastic crowd encircled the field, cheering on their team.

Shops reopened, and by sunset, the falafel men put out their woks and charcoal stoves to fry up the night's supply. The bean sellers did a booming trade. Fish sellers popped tiny fish into hot grease, scales, fins, eyes, and all. Once the fish were brown and crisp, they laid them on a paper to drain the oil. A line of containers stretched over several feet in readiness for the milk delivery. The afternoon delivery came in a pickup truck carrying large, silvery metal containers. The lid served as a measure. Customers identified their container and called out how many *ratuls* of milk they wanted. A *ratul* translated into a pint. Once we had it home, we had to strain it through cheesecloth to remove the dirt and cow hairs. Then we had to boil it to avoid getting TB. If we had been very industrious, we could have skimmed the cream off the top and made butter. We were not very industrious.

The drainage ditch provided a challenge for the local boys. They tried to jump across it without falling in. I'm not sure which was more difficult: jumping across when it was empty and risking falling down about four feet or jumping across when it was full of foul-smelling, black, inky sludge. There were small cement bridges over the ditch. The boys lined up bricks across width-wise and played ping-pong. If the ball went over the edge, well, retrieval depended on whether it was dry or full of water.

By 10:00 or 11:00 in the evening, people headed home. The night guards set up their *angareebs* or wooden beds with a thin cotton mattress placed over the webbing. They slept outside the shop doors to prevent robberies. On a hot night, they put the beds across the ditch to get the cooling evaporative effect of the water. The ditch provided a perfect breeding ground for mosquitoes, and Mogran had plenty of those. People slept covered with a sheet, from head to toe. Few bothered with a mosquito net. Most people slept outside under the stars. Only the crazy and "wealthy" foreigners slept inside the house with screens on the windows, the windows closed, under a mosquito net with an air cooler running. After all, who would want to miss the beautiful night sky, the hot dusty wind, and those noisy mosquitoes?

Love,

L

———————

Dear Harriet,

An American friend used to say, "You can't give directions to a Sudanese because the two of you aren't starting in the same place." I'm not sure if that is the reason, but it is difficult to communicate directions. I relate my location to a map and to landmarks. Since there were very few street names in English, most expatriates relied on special roundabouts or large buildings. As a driver, I noted different indicators than pedestrians did. One-way streets had different implications for drivers than for someone on foot. Those traveling by bus thought in terms of stations and the number or name of the stops. So, you can see that pedestrians and drivers could talk at cross-purposes. We used to joke about directions saying, "Go to the white wall with the green gate, watch for the woman in the red *tobe* and turn left at the chicken!"

Another characteristic of Africans is that they orient to directions like north, south, east, and west. They might say, "Go west along this road and then turn south." Well, whenever I try to get directions from the sun, it is high noon and I can discern only up and down. Frankly, I'm hopeless at directions. Lately, I've found African city dwellers are less aware of them as well.

One story that I heard early in my days in Africa took place in Kenya. A foreigner was walking along a path with a group of African men. One of them spotted a snake; so, he yelled, "Jump north!" The poor foreigner had no clue which way was north. I guess he had to "follow the leader."

In England, I tested out this theory of direction by asking a Ugandan woman where north was while standing deep in the London underground. She pointed north and then corrected for the solstice. I still do not know how she did it. Both women and men have the directions ingrained in their orientation, so it isn't a gender thing.

It was a useful reference, so I attempted to adopt it. For days, I practiced orienting myself as I drove around the city: south, west, southeast. I tried to restructure the map in my head to include directions and noted if a building was on the north or south side of the street. I thought I was doing well and felt pleased with myself. Soon I had occasion to give directions to a fellow foreigner and displayed my skill using north-south directions. The person stopped me to say they did not know which way was north or south. I guess I'm not the only one who is directionally challenged.

The point of this explanation is that we (foreigners) orient ourselves more by what the mapmakers tell us and less by noting geographical directions. The Africans didn't use a map, but they could get anywhere with surprising ease. They were aware of their surroundings because they live out of doors so much. We close ourselves up in our houses with our air conditioners and air coolers, read books, and stare at computer screens. The Africans sit outside, watch the stars and their neighbors, and talk to each other. We have a lot to learn from them about improving our awareness of nature, the world, and living in a community.

Love,

L

Dear Harriet,

Moving into Mogran drew us into that close-knit community. Once we moved in, a neighbor told us to see the Sheikh to get a ration card. He was available each evening after sunset prayers in the local primary school compound. We found him surrounded by several of our male neighbors. He welcomed us to Mogran and after a few polite exchanges, asked how many people were in our household. Peter M advised us to say five people: Acol (a-shoal), our house help, Peter M, our guard, an Anyua man, Janice, and me. I should explain we inherited our Anyua guard, who worked for the previous renter. It was marvelous to arrive at the local shop with our ration card and pick up enough sugar or bread for our needs.

A primary school was at the far end of our road. As we walked past the school, we often heard the children reciting their lessons in unison. Part of the wall had fallen down, so we could see the girls sitting at their desks in their uniforms. The boys' section must have been on the opposite side of the schoolyard. Typically, they segregate classes. When Peter M's family moved to Khartoum, he enrolled one of his daughters in that school. It had a positive reputation, and she did very well there.

In Mogran's better days, they had paved the roads. But by the time we came, dust and sand had buried the broken tarmac. We knew pavement was there when we didn't mire up in mud after a rain.

A view of the circular street near the gardens in Mogran

The 1988 floods damaged many houses in Mogran, and most of them had not been repaired. Every rainy season was a trial because the roofs leaked. Our house was no exception but was in better condition than many we saw. They developed our neighborhood in the 1950s. In its day, Mogran was a very desirable place to live because it was near the Nile and the city. Many influential people kept family homes in the area, even if they lived elsewhere in Khartoum.

There were several shops in the neighborhood. Yusef ran a small grocery on the corner. We picked up our sugar ration from there. His shop was handy if we needed sodas for guests. Yusef was also an estate agent, so whenever anyone wanted to rent a house in Mogran, he was your man!

The shops sold bread from the bakery half a mile from the house. The smell of freshly baked bread in the early morning hours enticed buyers. I enjoyed seeing them taking the long, thin loaves out of the huge ovens, while others ran with large trays of dough, ready to bake the next batch. When the loaves were done, they dumped them onto a line of sacking beside the road to cool. If we were making an early morning airport run, we stopped on our return to pick up bread for the day while it was hot and before it was dusty. Chris, my other neighbor, bought whole wheat flour from them. She made her own bread, but flour was not always easy to find. The bakers were generous.

Other things available from the shops included jams, tomato paste, baby formula, cans of fruit, instant coffee, loose tea, tea bags, milk powder, baking powder, cookies, and sodas. Besides prepackaged goods, there were tubs of lentils, chickpeas, cumin, and flour. Other shops sold Egyptian beans, the uncooked variety. The shopkeeper stood inside and the customers looked in from the outside (everyone except Chris, who went in and chose what she wanted!). There was limited space, so the counters across the front of the shop kept the customers out. They placed items available for sale on small shelves that lined three walls from floor to ceiling. In front of the shelves, they stacked loose goods. In the middle, the owner placed one or more large chest freezers that held sodas, yogurt, butter, and "white cheese" (feta). Sometimes they had bottles of sweetened milk. Sudanese don't drink plain milk, but prefer it sweetened. They have a serious sweet tooth!

Chris picked out what she wanted in a local shop

As the economy prospered in the late 90s, ice cream became a "hot item" in the shops. Most shops only had individual serving-sized packets, but we found one close by that sold it in a quart-sized plastic tub. It was nice ice cream and the plastic tub was useful too! There was not much variety in what grocery shops sold.

We tried to shop once a week. But if people didn't have a refrigerator, or liked the social interaction, they shopped daily. Mogran did not have a butcher or a fruit and vegetable stand. Several opened, but they didn't have adequate quality to satisfy the women in the community. Most people went to the market that was a mile from our house. The market had a good selection and, once they knew we lived in Mogran, they didn't hike the price. It was a small market, just four sections for vegetables, two for fruit, and three or four stalls for the butchers. More merchants sat under covered areas selling brooms, mats, spices, peanuts, small plastic bags of peanut butter (which was used as a flavoring in stews, not put on a sandwich). Sellers offering bluing proved popular. This item was essential in a country where almost everyone wears white and everything around them is brown. On the other side were small shops that specialized in beans of many varieties. I experimented with a few kinds, but never knew the best way to prepare the types available. Young boys sold plastic bags in several sizes. If I forgot mine, or bought more than I planned for, they sold me a bag to carry my goods home.

One of my favorite salesmen was the onion seller. He was a very jovial character who always asked what my favorite sports team was. How that got started, I don't recall. But we had a little chat when I stopped for onions. He got my attention because he had no legs. However, that disability didn't slow him down. He kept a plentiful supply of purple onions, measured out a generous number into his tins, and gave me a good price. He sat with his onions on the brown sacking on the ground and seemed to love what he was doing.

Love,

L

Dear Harriet,

In May 1990, Janice and I thought we had been shot out of a cannon on the literacy project. People couldn't wait to learn to read! We visited many places on the outskirts of Khartoum. Once two Cøllø Language Oversight Committee members accompanied us to see areas for potential classes. One had a nice school that parents had built. It had a mud wall seven feet high around it with locking gates. Inside were classrooms, shelters with reed mats on the top and sides, dirt floors, metal tables, benches and one to two chalkboards. Two rooms were for kindergarten, the rest for children by day with separate morning and afternoon sessions and for adults from 4:00 to 6:00. There was no electricity or running water. They said sixty-five teachers had signed up for the transition book course to begin in July!

We traveled south of Khartoum to Shejara "trees" and three large unplanned areas. Unplanned means that no one should live there because it is a desert with no extras. Men hauled water in drums on donkey carts from miles away. We met another committee member, a civil engineer, who took us to meet eight teachers. They didn't want to wait for our class in August. They selected a representative to come to our June class in Khartoum. Then he would train the others.

What people want are the adult primers, not just the English to Shilluk transition book. We haven't finished it yet, and plan to start on the primers after our holiday in July. Whew!

In addition to these visits, we were finishing the transition book and keyboarding 20 Lion Tales in Cøllø. Here's one story in English.

The Dog and the Fox

One day the Dog met with the Fox in the forest. The Dog asked the Fox, "What are you doing living in the forest? Why don't you settle in the village?"

The Fox said, "Will I have to work in the village?"

The Dog said, "The man gives me food." So, they went to the village.

The Dog entered the compound while the Fox waited outside. When the Dog took some food, the people beat him, so he ran back outside. The Fox asked him, "Why were you crying?"

Then the Dog said, "They were teaching me. That is why they beat me."

After that, the Fox refused village life. He ran to the forest and has stayed there ever since.

Love,

L

Dear Harriet,

We were getting our fuel when the attendant informed us that motor oil would be available later that day. There hadn't been any motor oil to buy for nine months. They told us to return at 10:00. We hurried off to tell our friends, but when we returned at 9:15, we were 105th in the queue. There were only ninety-one gallons available. If we had known, we could have signed up for one of them, but no one mentioned that. One problem with being a foreigner is that we miss out on vital information and lose chances. In the following weeks we got some.

Rauf from our office had an accident while riding his motorcycle. A man opened his car door at just the wrong time. It knocked Rauf off his bike, and he broke both bones in his left leg. The one who caused the accident took him to the hospital. The hospital insisted the driver find plaster to make a cast. He never found any, but Rauf knew a nurse, and she got some for him. However, when they x-rayed his leg, they found the doctor had not set the bones correctly. The cast had to come off and the bones reset. The X-ray machine was not in the surgery, so the doctor didn't know if he had set the bones properly or not. Further testing showed they were not set correctly, so they repeated the process again. Through these complications, Rauf remained cheerful.

Love,

L

Dear Harriet,

In most of Khartoum the electricity was only on for two to three hours per day. We rejoiced that we moved to Mogran because our house was on the line with the electricity company and the main water pumping station. So, if we were without power, the whole of Khartoum was without electricity and water. We had power twenty-four hours a day, and it made such a difference. I wished I could sit in front of my air cooler and not have to move. Temperatures in the house were over 100°F without it.

Computers were in their infancy in 1990, and while somewhat simpler, I did not know how to fix things that went wrong. While keyboarding a Cøllø storybook, I experimented with command keys. To my horror, I found that while words showed correctly on the screen, they didn't print out! I spent days working on the problem and convinced eleven pages to print correctly. Janice hadn't gotten used to the computer yet, so most of that ended up on my plate.

Love,

L

Dear Harriet,

I first met Esther when she visited her daughter in London. When I returned to live in Khartoum, Esther's husband, Amos, became the Chairman of the Cøllø Language Oversight Committee. He held this post for many years. I think I've mentioned that we often dropped by their house and visited the family. Esther is an intelligent, active person with a generous heart.

Many families struggled to feed their own families. But, as the war in the south continued, people fled to Khartoum for refuge. Upon arriving, they started looking for any relation, no matter how distant that relative might be. They hoped to stay with that household until they could get established. One person told me that they stopped taking people in when all the beds were full, even if their own children slept on the floor. A new bar of soap rarely lasted through the day. And the available food the nuclear family could afford barely provided one meal per day.

Should the family feed their children and themselves first, and then share whatever might be left? Did the family want to watch their guests starve? It was a challenging decision, but for the most part, food was shared with everyone. No one had enough, but no one starved. This is a good example of the sacrifices and the high value placed on community and the value of family in Sudan. Once I understood what was going on, my respect and admiration for my Sudanese friends only grew.

Esther went to Zambia for a nine-month course on Women's Development and when she returned, she found ways for women to earn money to support themselves. Many were widows because of the war and had several children to care for. They fled to the capital to avoid further violence from the forces that came through to terrorize the local population. However, after arriving in Khartoum, they discovered there were few jobs for illiterate women. The one skill that most of them had was brewing beer, an illegal activity under the Islamic *sharia* law. The product was in great demand. But when the police raided the house, they destroyed the equipment, poured the brew on the ground, and arrested the woman in charge. The court sentenced her to prison for weeks or months. She could take a small child or an infant with her, but the older children remained on their own with no adult supervision or provision. Esther wanted to offer a legal means of income generation and basic education.

Of course, Esther was not the only person seeking to help women in this way. There were several projects, each aimed at distinct groups, such as the Presbyterian Women, and ZagRags of Zagalona (for Nuba women). With two million refugees in the city, most of them women, there was no shortage of people to train. The problem was coming up with a new idea of what to make to capture the market. As soon as someone came out with a unique product, others copied it.

111

Quality control was another issue. One woman could make a wonderful product one day, but the next time, it might be of poor quality. The women needed money, so if they didn't have time to do it well, they brought what they could do. They pressured the organizers to pay them for their efforts regardless of the quality because they had a tale of disaster for which she needed money. I'm not implying that the stories were not true, but the result is the same. If you can't keep up the quality, it is hard to sell the product. If you can't sell the product, there is no money to pay the workers.

Esther started a sewing center using treadle machines. The outlying areas had no electricity, so these were useful. The women made school uniforms and men's shirts. Then they started tie-dyeing material and making various items of clothing. Other indigenous skills including basket weaving, decorating gourds, and beadwork. Eventually, they began crochet and embroidery and as the women's skills were honed, they produced lovely things.

One of the women stringing tiny beads to make a bracelet

Crafts on display for a sale on our verandah

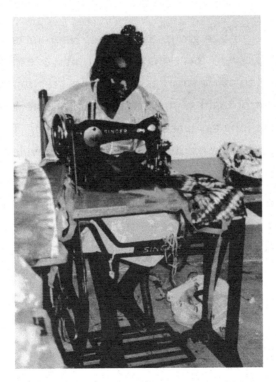

A woman using a treadle sewing machine

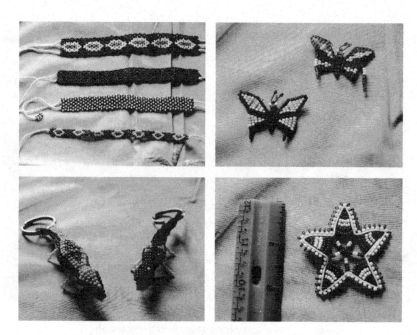

Bracelets, butterflies, crocodiles, and a star for Christmas

Esther registered her group as the Self Help Society. They had small shops in several locations, but the rent was expensive. In the end, they had to move to areas of town not frequented by expatriates. I often brought items home to sell in the USA. Customs didn't mind as long as I wasn't bringing in clothing. The beadwork and pillow covers were duty-free to help the "developing world."

The US and European markets were important because, as you know, tourists rarely traveled to Sudan. It was difficult to get a visa, and the people who came had a serious reason for staying there, either for aid work or business, but not to have a vacation. Despite these challenges, Esther, and those like her, changed the lives of many people.

Love,

L

Dear Harriet,

I'm not sure I've mentioned this before, but the Cøllø have a king (*rädh*). Nyikangø was the founder of the Cøllø nation. According to Struck (Westermann, LI), African dynasties typically lasted 13.5 years. He multiplied 29 by 13.5 since there have been 28 to 30 known descendant kings from Nyikangø. The result suggested that the Cøllø kingdom began during the first quarter of the sixteenth century. Here is the story I received in Cøllø.

Nyikangø, as the eldest son, was in line to be named chief. But when the time came, they chose a cowardly man who never left the village to hunt. They describe this person as *"opaj."*

Nyikangø's wife, Angweedø, suggested he look for his own chieftainship. Nyikangø hesitated to go alone on such a venture, so his wife suggested he take along his cousins, Ojwøk and Ojuli, and their families. After discussing it, everyone agreed. They traveled together until they came to the small village of Thurø, near Wau in Bahr al-Ghazal in the southwest of Sudan.

While there, Nyikangø married the chief's daughter, Akej. When the chief died, his daughter inherited his title. Since Nyikango was married to the new chief, the people of Thurø wanted to kill him. So the family fled further east.

By the time they arrived at Tungø, Nyikangø had despaired of finding a chieftainship. Many Anyuak people lived around Tungø, and Nyikangø found good hunting and fishing. Leadership was the only problem. The Funj were in charge, but no one knew where they originated. The Anyuak wanted to break free of their rule.

One day, the elders of the Anyuak people came to Nyikangø complaining that the Funj did not know how to rule well. They had seen Fur people come from the north to spy on them and feared their intentions. They suggested that Nyikangø and his people join forces with them to get rid of these other people groups. Nyikangø made them promise to pay tribute if he helped defeat their enemies. The Anyuak agreed. After a significant struggle, Nyikangø, his people and the Anyuak defeated the Funj at Nyilwal. After that, people got along well, as Nyikangø proved to be a talented administrator.

As Nyikangø grew older, he became more vulnerable to attack and depended on his warrior son, Dak, for help. Foreigners attacked Nyikangø's village, and Dak had to rescue him. Once Dak helped defeat the enemy, the story uses the phrase: *Ki bang menani, amag thøl piny* which means "And after that, they put down the rope." Cøllø people tie a rope to a stake and drive it into the ground. They believe God lives under the ground and tying the rope to the stake allows them to tie the spirit of God to that place. During this period, they made circular houses using the smooth hunting spear to draw the outline for the house.

Life passed peacefully until someone died in Nyikangø's village. Dak had been out hunting. When he returned, he found a freshly dug grave in front of his house. He asked, "Who died?" The neighbors informed him someone in Nyikangø's village had died, but they buried the person at Dak's house. Dak believed this action brought uncleanness; so, he moved his family further east to Panyidwey, near the Sobat River and made a small village. (I lived in Panyidwey or Doleib Hill for my brief stay in the village.)

Nyikangø was not happy with this sudden move and challenged Dak. He said, "Why did you make a village for a small boy? The kingdom was yours! Why did you move away?" Perhaps Nyikango had provoked Dak to leave by burying this person in front of his house. But he continued to complain about Dak's departure. They argued. Dak refused to return, so Nyikangø gave the chieftainship to Dinyø, his son who lived in Tonga.

Another son, Bwør, was not married, so Nyikangø gave him Dak's mother, Akej, to be his wife. They lived in Nyikangø's village, Paluko. This action enraged Dak, who planned to kill Bwør. Nyikangø advised Bwør that when Dak came, he should embrace Dak as if he were embracing his wife. These sexual advances would shock Dak, so he would leave. The trick worked, and Dak returned to his village. Bwør then married his cousin Nyidway, and they had two children.

That is how the kingship started. From Nyikangø's three sons, Dinyø, Dak, and Bwør, came three branches of the family. The kingship rotates among the three. The son chosen to be king must have been born while his father was king, but can only become king after the other two families have had their turns.

Love,

L

Dear Harriet,

Our first visit with the king (*rädh*) was in April 1990. One of his wives had died six weeks before, and it was time for her funeral rites, also known as *ywög*. They invited Janice and me to attend the occasion in Hai Jusef on the outskirts of Khartoum. The king had moved to Khartoum because of the war. People consulted with him whenever they needed to solve a problem or dispute. On this occasion, people hired buses to get to Hai Jusef, and there must have been over 1000 people present. Each village had its own flag and waved it with enthusiasm as they danced.

The women dressed in their best clothes and a *lawø*. A *lawø* is a two-yard-long piece of cloth tied on the right shoulder. Men tie their *lawø* on the left shoulder to keep the right arm free for spear throwing. Everyone wore a belt. I asked why since I'd never seen people wear belts on other occasions. They explained that traditionally they must be prepared to go to war. Their clothing should not get in the way when fighting. Many women wore bells on their ankles made from Pepsi bottle tops strung on a string. They jangled loudly. The women and a handful of the men sported headdresses that resembled a lion's mane. Everyone carried a stick. Since wood is in short supply, fluorescent light tubes served the same purpose.

As we walked around enjoying the dancing and the energy, we came to a large square filled with people. They were sitting down and chorusing "Wöö," meaning "our Father." The center of their attention was the king, who pronounced a blessing on the people. He was wearing a giraffe mane crown and the traditional pink cloth (*lawø*). Cøllø soldiers and his advisors surrounded him.

One of our committee members appeared out of nowhere and asked, "Would you like to take the king's picture?"

"Of course!" Off he went to arrange it.

Before we could say "Pepsi bottle tops," we were being presented to him. I forgot every appropriate word they had ever taught me to say to him over the past five years. Janice did not know what to do, so she bowed. He responded graciously to our lack of court experience and moved to a better position in relation to the sun for our photos.

We learned that the king never looks back. So, it was with great interest that we watched him sit down. He backed up until he was standing on the leopard skin rug in front of his chair. Then someone positioned the chair behind him. That person wouldn't have his job for long if he allowed the king to crash to the ground.

Rädh Aney

We assume a king will wear a crown, and the Cøllø king is no exception. However, instead of gold or silver, they form the mane of the giraffe into a circlet for his crown. The king has special rights to any giraffe that is intentionally or accidentally killed. The hunter must report the incident immediately or pay a fine. Tradition says he gets to use the parts of the giraffe, though I expect he shares the meat once he has what he needs. The mane and the tail are of particular value.

After our meeting, people escorted us to a house where we relaxed. Shortly, a man entered the room and everyone stood up, including us! I was not going to miss that clue again (as I had with the Sudanese ambassador in Nairobi). He turned out to be the Cøllø equivalent to the Prime Minister. He had worked as a medical technician before being promoted to this position, and he spoke excellent English. We asked questions, and he explained what we were seeing. He pointed out that he wore a necklace with three strands of beads. As with many symbols, the number of strands showed his high status. Those wearing two strings or one string had lower status. So, I asked if the king wore four strands.

The prime minister laughed, as did everyone else! "No," he explained. "The *rädh* wears a single strand of ivory beads." Men also wear a ring of ivory on their upper left arm.

Later, we met the Minister for Relief and Rehabilitation. Once again, I realized that my training for this job had failed to cover some crucial topics. Suggestions on protocol with prominent officials, public relations, and how to dress when meeting royalty would be helpful.

We wandered out once more to see what was happening. We came upon the *rädh*, only this time, we tried to blend into the crowd as important guests were being presented while television cameras captured the moment. As the meeting finished, these guests departed. One of them headed straight over to us. We greeted him, noting he was a Muammar Qaddafi look-alike. Sure enough, he was the Libyan ambassador, and he wanted to greet us, the only white people he could find.

Once we returned home, we collapsed. It was an eventful and exhausting day.

Love,

L

Dear Harriet,

No doubt you recall our two cats, Garang and Sadiq. The Cølløs believe cats have something to do with the spirits of their ancestors. So, while they keep them to catch snakes, they don't want to touch them. Our cats didn't consider the Cølløs' preferences and insisted on being petted by whomever was available.

Garang, the orange and white tabby, loved to find an unsuspecting Cøllø man sitting in a chair. She hopped into his lap and stretched out across him for her full and considerable length. Janice or I found the man with his hands in the air speaking to her. "Get down!" We tried to push her from behind to encourage her to move. (It is improper to scoop her up out of a gentleman's lap.) Garang turned into gelatin with not a solid part in her body. She just lay there, enjoying our consternation until she decided to leave. Then she collected herself and jumped off, but only when she was ready.

Sadiq, the "green" cat, loved to leap onto the desk where the men were working. She rubbed her head on their pencils and tried to get them to stroke her and rub her ears. The Cølløs didn't want to touch her when she stretched out across the workspace and any papers they had. She spread a thick layer of dust over everything, since rolling in the dirt was one of her other favorite activities.

The Cølløs always called her "green," and I couldn't work out why. So, I asked, "What is green? Are her eyes green?" (I thought they were.)

"No, her fur is green."

Well, I had never seen any animal with green fur, so I pursued this further. "What would you call her in Cøllø?" I asked.

"*Nyawnyang.*" That explained it, I guess. *Nyaw* is the word for "cat" and *nyang* means "crocodile." So, she was a crocodile-colored cat. Apparently, crocodiles are green.

Sadiq had one other talent that I'd never seen before. She talked to the birds. She had mastered their language well because we often saw her lying on the verandah, meowing in a funny way. Each time, there was a small bird perched on the top of the column, chirping back. Soon, the cat convinced it to come down for a closer discussion of a more secret nature. When the bird did so, the inevitable happened. Bird feathers went everywhere. She must have had a good line!

Garang caught birds and other small animals in the normal way. Once, I saw her trying to talk with them while lying on the top of the compound wall. She did not know the language well, so she soon returned to pouncing on them.

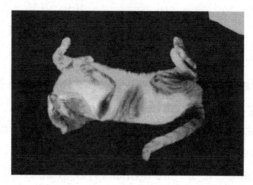

Garang in one of her favorite poses

Love,

L

Dear Harriet,

Janice and I had met Chris at church. She was the head of the primary section of Unity High School. She had been living with Wanda, but Wanda had to leave the country to care for her parents. Having checked out the other third of our house, we thought Chris would enjoy it. There was a huge verandah for her plants. She easily divided the main room into two, so there was a bedroom and living room. The enclosed verandah served as her kitchen. She was delighted with the place and moved in. It proved to be beneficial for all of us, especially as she was on a different electricity phase. So, if our power was out, we could borrow hers, and vice versa. We removed the gate between our backyards and moved freely between our two homes. Her house had an outdoor toilet and shower, but she didn't mind that.

Chris is English, and she and Janice trained me well on British customs, particularly around Christmas time. Mince pies became a favorite. She was involved with the Nuba Mountain community based in Khartoum. She worked with a Nuba woman to form the Zagalona women's cooperative. They did tie-dyeing and sewing. Then Chris sold their products in Khartoum and England.

She is one of those thin, wiry women with far more energy than I could imagine. Everything she did, whether cooking, sewing, entertaining, or teaching, she did in a quarter of the time it took me. I've had a few women in my life like that, Pam and Chris being two of them. I tried to keep up, but decided my brain works at a different speed. She remains an inspiration and a good friend.

Love,

L

Dear Harriet,

The botanical gardens were in a large, round section of Mogran behind the Agricultural Bank. If the gates were open, I walked along an avenue lined with lovely trees and plants from all over Sudan. There were surprises throughout the garden: an old wooden water wheel, a latticework arbor, and graceful palm trees. A nursery near the entrance sold plants. A large fence protected the outside of the garden, with bougainvillea growing behind it. This plant thrives in Sudan. There were also several acacia trees with inch-long thorns. It was best to walk away from the fence so as not to be stabbed by them. The overall temperature of Mogran was several degrees cooler because of this extensive garden. At 121°F in the shade, two or three degrees might not sound like a lot. But, when we drove off the tarmac road onto the dirt circle around the garden, we could feel the coolness on our skin. It was a lovely sensation.

Inch-long thorns on an acacia tree

The houses in Mogran, as in most of Khartoum, had walls around them. The residents maintained the grounds inside those walls. Unfortunately, the Sudanese took little notice of the outside of their houses. The streets became littered with banana peels, plastic bags, and even discarded feet from an unfortunate goat.

Half an hour before the garbage truck showed up, a man walked down the street, blowing a whistle. He alerted us to get our trash out to the street for collection. Then the workers came to grab the baskets or drums of refuse and toss it into a slow-moving vehicle. Often, the papers thrown into the open truck bed got loose and flew around the street. We burned our papers so our neighbors didn't read them. One friend said the garbage collectors should be called "garbage distributors."

One afternoon as I walked home, I saw the garbage men taking a break in the heat of the day under a large tree. The truck was close by and they were sifting through the items people had thrown away, to see if any was worth keeping. They found little of interest from our house as our employees picked out things before they ever made it to the rubbish bin. Once trash blew onto the street, it stayed there. No one seemed concerned that the neighborhood resembled the start of a landfill. So, it was with relief that we got word via Peter M that the Sheikh and the local council had ordered everyone to clean the space outside their compound. If they didn't do so by a certain time, they would be fined. It was a great incentive, and our neighbors responded positively. The street looked much better.

Our neighbor Chris was having building work done in her house. This entailed having a large pile of sand near the street. Unfortunately, the council considered this as garbage, and we were about to be fined if it didn't go away. She paid a few young boys to carry buckets of sand out to the road to fill in holes, at least temporarily. That made the way more drivable and got rid of the pile just in the nick of time.

Love,

L

Dear Harriet,

The Gulf War, when Iraq invaded Kuwait, was going on during this time. The Sudanese government sided with Iraq, which put everyone on edge. No one wanted to make a big display because of the tension. So, when our students graduated from the transition book class, the closing ceremony needed to be a low-key affair. The committee sent invitations to significant members of the local community to witness the presentations. We served candy and Pepsi. The committee members took an active role, as we were too busy with other work to organize these events.

The Alphabet Book was ready to go to the printer, but we had no money. I wrote several proposals, but most embassies and organizations were fed up with the government and had decided not to give money to anything. Each one faced the moral dilemma of facilitating a government that continued to destroy the people the organization wanted to help. When contracts ended, many agencies left Sudan for that reason. We needed $3,000. James' storybook needed to be printed, but we had no money for that either. The British ambassador gave us a gift of $2,000, and we sent the Alphabet Book to the printer.

Love,

L

Dear Harriet,

Events can trigger interesting phrases that just stick with me. One of these phrases is: "Every day, but not some." Let me tell you what happened. Our Cøllø literacy manager, Nyikwec, lived in the far reaches of Hai Jusef and we finished work late. We had a reasonable supply of fuel, so Janice offered to take him home. They bounced along the road for half an hour before arriving at his compound. Nyikwec pointed out their neighbor had a "fold-down-seat bus," one of the medium-sized buses used for public transport. The drivers fill up the proper seats, and then starting from the back, passengers fold down a seat in the aisle, hence our name for it.

Anyway, back to the story. He told Janice that sometimes his neighbor let them ride with him into town in the mornings. Janice asked, "Does he go into town every day?"

"Oh, yes," Nyikwec replied, "every day, but not some."

The longer we lived in Sudan, the more apt this phrase became until I added this saying to my repertoire.

I was working at my desk while Janice met with the teachers. I heard a knock on the gate. I ignored it at first, but they were insistent. The men collecting the garbage were selling black plastic garbage bags at four for thirty cents. People scarcely had enough money to eat, and the sanitation department was selling plastic garbage bags! I bought a few and used them, but they never offered them again.

About a week later, I saw Peter M talking to someone at the gate. I inquired who it was and what they wanted. He explained that the supervisor from the sanitation department asked if they collected the garbage every day.

"What did you tell him?"

"I said they came every day because they come twice a week!" (Every day, but not some... strikes again).

Love,

L

Dear Harriet,

I wouldn't want you to think life was all work and no play in Sudan. There were occasional picnics on the banks of one of the Niles. The

Blue Nile flowed faster and was less muddy. People said there was bilharzia (a very unpleasant parasite) in the White Nile, so that was a less popular destination. The children loved building sandcastles, playing frisbee, and even flying kites. They enjoyed sliding down the bank into the water or digging tunnels in the mud and sand.

Children playing in the sand on the banks of the Blue Nile

The other place I frequented for relaxation was the American Club, now renamed the International Club. Clubs served an important purpose as there were not many places to relax and sit around on a hot day in a swimsuit. The Sudan Club served the British community. The American Club was open to the American and Canadian communities, though they welcomed other nationalities. There was also the German Club, the Greek Club, and the Syrian Club. The Sudan Club first ran into difficulties during the Gulf War. Sudan sided with Iraq against Kuwait. With coalition troops fighting in the Gulf, many British and American residents felt safer away from Sudan. With a reduced number of British members, the Sudan Club opened its doors to Europeans (that is, from the European community). However, as an American, they required me to have at least five members vouch for me before I joined. I just paid the guest fee and tagged along with Janice as she was a member.

The Sudan Club had a very British menu for lunch: shepherd's pie, Cornish pasty, and trifle for dessert. The atmosphere was pleasant, with lots of grass, trees, and lovely flowers. They had a postage-stamp-size pool shaded by large trees. They had a squash court, but I've never been adept at games that required one to hit a ball, so I didn't take advantage of that. The waiters wore long caftan robes and never appeared to age or change.

The American Club had a much larger pool surrounded by concrete and bordered by a train track. We heard the trains go by but couldn't see them because of the cement block security wall. The line of twenty changing rooms served as a sound barrier. I'm not sure why they needed so many. Three outside showers were handy, but only one gave water at a time. The management put up a modesty wall so bathers could shower with only their heads visible. Inside the Ladies or Gents, there were proper showers and changing rooms. Tables near the pool had sunshades. Customers could sit in the shade while sipping their *kerkedeh* (a drink made from hibiscus) or eating their burger and fries. There was a tiny garden and a small lawn near the entrance. One side had a large tennis/basketball court and a playground for children. After a few years, the American Club Board decided to build a wading pool. It was a good idea, but it was deeper than it should have been. Parents had to stay close to the smaller children so they didn't get in over their heads.

The American Club pool

The menu at the club stayed the same for most of my twenty-two years there, even when reprinted in newer and flashier formats. Often the promised fare was unavailable, even though the ingredients were in the market. I ordered a beef or chicken kebab with chips (French fries) and a jug of the most wonderful grapefruit juice I've ever tasted. My favorite waiter, Ibrahim, always knew what my preferences were and when I wanted the food. I arrived, found a table, and signaled to Ibrahim. He brought the menu, took my order, and gave me time for a swim before he brought my drink or my food. If I swam too long, he called me and, if I still delayed, covered my food with another plate to keep off the flies. I tipped him well.

Love,

L

Dear Harriet,

Let me tell you about Ramadan, a very significant month of the year. The five pillars of Islam are the acts a Muslim must do to earn favor with God. They are: acknowledging God is one God and Muhammed is his last prophet, praying five times a day, fasting from dawn to dusk during the month of Ramadan, showing concern for and giving to the poor, and going on pilgrimage to Mecca, known as the *Hajj*. It is very important for devout Muslims to practice these things throughout their lives.

We had settled into our Mogran house when Ramadan rolled around again. Ramadan was in June when I first arrived in Sudan in 1982, but it moves ahead fifteen days every year. By 1990, Ramadan began in the winter. Ramadan had not affected us in Fitihab, but we experienced a shock in Mogran!

Janice and I were sleeping until clashes and clangs and the sound of boys chanting and singing woke us at 3:30 a.m. We didn't know what was happening. I leapt out of bed and found Janice at the door ahead of me. She peered into the darkness with a worried look on her face. The warnings of a *coup d'état* entered our minds. As the noise continued, the penny dropped that these young men were the neighborhood alarm clocks. They got up early and formed a gang of noisemakers, bringing along pot lids and metal spoons, drums and whatever else made a noise. They beat those while calling it was time to get up and have "supper," the last meal allowed before fasting began. People often enjoy oatmeal porridge and, of course, a swig or two of water.

The boys stood outside each house until a light came on, showing they were awake. Then they moved along to the next place. We heard them moving up and down every street, alerting the whole of Mogran. They did not ignore our house. They delighted in trying to awaken us. We were not fasting and had no wish to get up at 3:30 in the morning. They never got a tip from us at the end of Ramadan! I thought of tipping them at the beginning to skip our house.

Some years they were more regular than others. The boys only overslept three days out of the month that year. By 2004, we didn't hear them at all. I suppose people had invested in alarm clocks, so the young men's racket was no longer essential.

I've given Ramadan a good deal of thought. Fasting as a community is a very unifying experience. That differs from the private Christian fasting. With the Muslims, going through it together makes it more bearable since it lasts for an entire month, and no one knows how long that month will be. When the authorities in Saudi Arabia see the new moon, then Ramadan has ended.

I used to think the hardest conditions of Ramadan were not eating and drinking. Not drinking is the most difficult, especially when the weather is hot. But the next worst thing is sleep deprivation. In theory, everyone should work during the day and then eat, drink, and sleep at night. As the month wears on, people become active at night and sleep during the day. The universities and schools cancel classes, and secretaries use their typewriters as pillows. Forget having papers processed, as officials rarely turned up at the office. Those who tried to carry on as usual got less and less sleep. Work normally stops at 2:00 in the afternoon, so there's time to sleep. The call to prayer and breakfast comes at dusk, about 6:20 p.m. After breakfast, men go to pray at the mosque or receive visitors. The market springs to life as many enjoy the cool of the evening and the extra "goodies" on sale during this special season. About midnight, people return home and have "lunch" and catch a couple of hours of sleep before being awakened for "supper" in the early morning hours. By dawn, men go to pray, or sleep a few more minutes before getting up for work.

During my first year in Sudan, I received an invitation to a Ramadan *fatuur* (breakfast). Naturally, I thought our neighbors would invite us in Fitihab and Mogran, but such was not the case. The economy had taken a serious downturn with a severe recession. The value of the Sudanese pound dropped from £s 1.25 / $1.00 in 1982 to £s 2,000 / $1.00 by 1993. Few had salaries or pensions adjusted for inflation, and so money didn't go very far. My friends Pastor Peter and Rachel (along with Acol) earned £s20,000 ($100) in a month. With eight children in the household, their basic monthly expenses were £s22,200. They had nothing extra as they could barely meet their needs, even with everyone employed. What hope did the other households have with only one person working? As a result, inviting guests to share a meal became a rarity.

Love,

L

Dear Harriet,

Early in my stay in Khartoum, other expatriates cautioned me not to give money to the many children begging on the streets. More and more families fled to the capital for safety. Men fought in the civil war, leaving their wives to figure out how to feed the family. Young boys resorted to begging for food or coins. I had no way of knowing who was in need or part of a racket. Similar to Dickens' *A Tale of Two Cities*, unscrupulous adults used children to beg on the streets to bring back money. If they failed, beatings were common. The "Fagans" manipulated homeless children that were desperate to survive. Other children sniffed glue or petrol to escape from their misery. I expect every child has his or her own story. More rarely, we saw an older man or woman begging, especially during Ramadan.

Janice and I stopped at a red light near the university during Ramadan. An older man approached us, asking for a handout. As we were still new to the city, we didn't give him anything. His face contorted in anger, and I suspect he cursed us as we drove away. We had committed a faux pas, and I was determined to find out how to follow the custom, without giving money. I bought roasted peanuts in little plastic bags. When approached by anyone in need, I opened the glove box and got out a bag. Everyone looked happy to receive them, unless they worked for a gang. Gang members only wanted money. One boy pushed the peanuts away and showed me he wanted cash! So, I said, "If you don't want the peanuts, give them back!" He did, and I drove away. On another occasion, the boy accepted the food but said, "We need more than food." That was true enough, and I noticed the peanuts went stale. So, after that, I started carrying around squares of locally made soap. It was cheap, useful, and didn't deteriorate. Almost everyone cheerfully received this offering.

Seventy days after Ramadan is the *Hajj* that takes place during *Eid el-Adha* (the feast of sacrifice). In former times, people traveled across Africa, especially from Nigeria through Sudan, to get to the Arabian Peninsula. That journey must have been fraught with unimaginable difficulties, and many pilgrims never made it back home. Instead, they settled in Sudan. Today, there are many Hausa and Fulani peoples living within the borders of Sudan.

Even in recent times, it took significant effort. Just getting the visa was a challenge. As soon as Ramadan was over, the applications started. Each year, Saudi Arabia sets limits on how many travelers can come from any one country. These restrictions allow pilgrims from different countries to fulfill this obligation. You may have read about the deaths that occur from stampedes during the *Hajj*. There are huge numbers of people in a small space and if someone gets excited, it can cause a panic. So, the government tries to control the total number of pilgrims, hoping to minimize the risks.

Once the visa is in hand, one can book a flight. Airlines schedule special flights across the Red Sea to Saudi Arabia. Officials used a different terminal at the airport just for the *Hajj* passengers. The check-in time was six hours for those flights. "Why?!" I asked. Most people have never flown before, so when they get on the plane, everyone sits in the front row. It takes that many hours to have each one in their correct seat with their seatbelt fastened.

When we visited our former landlord, Abdul, after his pilgrimage, he displayed the large white towel he wore while marching around the *Kabba* or black stone. We asked him what he had learned through this experience and his answer was surprising. He mentioned how wonderful it was to see the beautiful buildings and the great works completed in the past. Maybe it was the language barrier or the way we phrased the question. I thought his answer would describe a spiritual experience. Still, it had been a momentous occasion in his life.

Love,

L

Dear Harriet,

Our household provided breakfast on the verandah around 10:00 a.m. on workdays. We continued the practice during Ramadan. We could do whatever we chose in our compound. So, Acol either cooked a meal or prepared beans purchased the night before. Sudanese traditionally have *fuul* beans (Egyptian beans) with tomatoes, onions, sesame seed oil, and cumin. Peter bought fresh bread each morning. Our numbers increased during this period, as we were one of the few places southerners could find something to eat. It pleased us when they announced the last days of Ramadan, and we looked forward to the *Eid el-Fitr* or "breakfast feast."

Ramadan ended when the mosque broadcast cries of *"Allah hu Akbar"* (God is great) and *"la Illah illa Allah"* (there is no God but Allah) over and over and over for hours. A long queue of people at the mosque wanted to take part in this continual chorus. The various imams and muezzins had a turn. Fathers and sons called together, or sometimes a group of boys. They joined the first group for a couple of rounds to get the rhythm, then the first group dropped out and the second carried on for a while. Then the next group took up the chant in an unbroken refrain. This lasted for much of the morning until the volunteers felt they had done their part and took a well-deserved break.

Everyone dressed up in their best new clothes, as Christians do on Christmas or Easter. There were small Ferris wheels set up in parks for the children and other special entertainment. The community had fulfilled its obligation to God and bonded together. It was now time to celebrate and get their days and nights sorted out. The feast lasts for three days. Many people travel home to visit family and don't make it back to work for several more. By the middle of the month after Ramadan, things returned to normal.

Love,

L

Dear Harriet,

By December 1990, we had sixty-four students studying our materials in Egypt and more than that in Khartoum. We decided we had "lift off." While Janice and I were on a break for Christmas, the teachers said they would meet to decide the next steps for the project. They promised to have lots of work for us when we returned. That was music to my ears.

One disturbing piece of news was that James, the lead teacher, was arrested. They never brought charges against him, but tortured and imprisoned him. We learned that someone in his compound (similar to a small apartment complex) had dealings with the rebel movement and the security people had their eyes on him. When they came, they arrested everyone in the place, James included. The next day, they released the women. Several neighbors came to find out what had happened, and the security officers arrested them as well.

They beat James badly, and he had trouble walking. We heard he was unwell and might go to a hospital. At least people could visit him there. Our director said it was better that we stay away as we might attract more attention to the project, and that would not remove suspicion from James.

He was released, for which we were very thankful. However, he feared meeting with any expatriates for obvious reasons. We agreed to connect with him inside Amos' home. That arrangement worked, and we continued our language development activities.

It took a couple of months before James felt free to visit us. He told us he suffered greatly during his arrest. They hit him in the throat so much he couldn't eat for seven days. They burned him on the stomach and refused to release him until the burns had healed. No doctors or medicines were allowed. They stood on his ankles and knees to beat him, so those places continued to give him pain. The security people went through his things and took what they wanted, including his clothes, shoes, and watch. I brought him an old watch from my dad, and he was thrilled. Janice found him a shirt. He was afraid to sleep in the same house two nights in a row. His friends offered to help him since he had no money. On a positive note, he was excited to see his books ready for printing and wanted to work. He thanked everyone who prayed for him.

Love,

L

Chapter 4:
1991

Dear Harriet,

Daytime temperatures in the winter months ranged between 70 and 80. If it were this cool through the year, how wonderful it would be. Since Janice and I had arrived in Sudan in February, that became the month we did our annual planning. The only problem with that was that February is in the winter, and most of the year is summer. By the time we got to May, we asked ourselves, *How could we have thought we could get all that done in this heat?*

We began having visa problems as the government dissolved our former sponsor, the Council for the South. We had applied to renew our residence visas. When the officer saw who our sponsor was, he said, "That Council has been dissolved. They can't sponsor visas!"

Russ, our administrator, rushed around trying to find a new sponsor while leaving the passports at immigration. We mentioned at our regular language committee meeting that we might have to leave because we couldn't renew our visas. The members said, "It is very important for you to stay. We will get your papers renewed. The work can go on much faster if you are here. We will go to Pio (a Cøllø member of the Revolutionary Council) and tell him that our team is here, and we want them to stay!"

One man was dispatched to see Pio. Amos phoned our office on Sunday to ask where our papers were because Pio was going to see to our visas personally! We were relieved that at last we had a working phone in our office.

Sure enough, we got our visas renewed, even though finding the new sponsor took two months. Our office staff did an amazing job so I could concentrate on the Cøllø work. The National Council for the Education of Refugees and Displaced Southern Students became our new sponsor. Try to get that on a rubber stamp!

Love,

L

Dear Harriet,

Historically, within SIL, the financial expectation was that expatriates assigned to a language group raised the money from their supporters to fund the work. So, when translators needed a salary or they wanted to print books, the expatriates raised the money. We worked with a community of three-quarters of a million people! While Janice and I provided breakfast and office space along with a computer and printer, there was no way we could regularly pay the fifty or more teachers transport money. Besides, the laws of Sudan viewed those payments not as incentive, but as salary. If teachers showed receipts to the court, we could be liable for all kinds of payments. We had one guard who lived in a building on the property. He sued us for transport money and won! We had to be very careful.

Times were challenging, so the committee wanted to pay incentives to the teachers to help them. The Nile was very low, so Blue Nile Dam generated little power. There was a shortage of fuel, so the government rationed it. Medicines were not available. So, we needed to help them. We spent an average of $58/week on food. That is the average monthly wage for a Sudanese. James' university only paid him $33/month. During this time, I learned the good African saying, "Ask, you might get." I learned how to write funding proposals, and we requested $1,000 from different organizations, including the Sudan Council of Churches, so we could offer incentives. We knew we wouldn't get that amount, but we might receive something.

Along with our teachers, we produced the following materials from March 1990 to March 1991:

- The English to Shilluk Transition Book (94 students completed classes)
- The Alphabet Storybook
- 20 Folktales
- 50 Shilluk Riddles
- Pre-primer (a sight word story book)
- 1991 calendar
- Alphabet Chart

Through 1991, we continued to work on the Alphabet Storybook, a book of fifty proverbs, a 1992 calendar, a history of the Cøllø kings, and the primer.

The Cøllø Language Oversight Committee decided the Cølløs in Khartoum needed to understand the new writing system. They planned Enlightenment Meetings first in Fitihab. We planned to go, but Kent had our car looking for tires. He returned at 2:00 p.m., so we didn't make the meeting. In a way, I'm glad. They are exhausting, and I was tired from a three-and-a-half-hour committee meeting the previous day. It is important for them to discuss these

141

issues among themselves, as it is their language, not ours. James presented the various topics and did a great job.

Love,

L

Dear Harriet,

One of my supporting churches requested a letter from my supervisor. Russ agreed to write it, and here is part of what he said.

"Leoma and her partner Janice are working on the Shilluk language. Shilluk has baffled missionaries, linguists, and anthropologists for many decades. Back in the 1940s and 50s, missionaries tried to write Shilluk and even did some Bible translation. Unfortunately, the language, particularly the sound system, was so difficult that the translations they did are virtually unusable. The alphabet they chose just doesn't make any sense of the language. Leoma, after seven years of extensive research, finally broke into the sound system and has developed an alphabet which is nothing short of a milestone. Her work in Shilluk, a Nilotic language, is going to be a benchmark work for all other missionaries working on Nilotic languages. Those languages represent many, many millions of people.

"Leoma and Janice are up to their eyebrows in literacy work at this time. Since developing the alphabet, they have been busy producing books, primers, calendars, and other reading materials in Shilluk. The Shilluk alphabet was just too difficult. Now that they have a readable alphabet, it is really great to see the high level of excitement and motivation this has had among the Shilluks. They are pressing for a new, readable translation of the Bible. They really want it."

Love,

L

Dear Harriet,

We rarely had two days alike, but here is an example of one day.

The Plan:

6:30 a.m.: Get up, feed cats, make coffee, listen to the news, have a time of Bible reading and prayer, take down the mosquito net, put ice and water in the large thermos, buy our ration of bread, and put it in plastic bags to keep it from drying out, fill up the water filter, put clothes in the washing machine, and pray for electricity and water.

8:00 a.m.: Make headway on updating the dictionary on the computer until time for breakfast at 9:00.

8:30 a.m.: Acol, our house help, arrives.

9:00 a.m: Eat breakfast.

10:00 a.m.: Work at Amos' with James until 2:00.

3:00 p.m.: Eat lunch. Acol goes home.

3:45-5:00 p.m.: Siesta and listen to the news.

5:30-7:30 p.m.: Input corrections worked out with James earlier.

8:00 p.m.: Eat supper.

8:30-9:30 p.m.: Play Boggle (we are becoming addicted to it).

9:30–10:30 p.m.: Prepare for bed, put up the mosquito net. My bedroom doubles as the office, so I have to tidy up. Lights out at 10:30.

Changes that happened:

9:00 a.m.: Richard arrives to check out our air coolers, which need maintenance before the coming hot season. As he drinks some water, we discuss the latest events in the Gulf and implications for life in Sudan. While we are engaged in this conversation, Peter M arrives. He apologizes for not coming to work the previous day. He has been sick.

9:30 a.m.: I show Richard the air coolers and discuss what needs to be done. Janice talks with Peter and then cooks our breakfast, makes sandwiches for James and another man who will be at the meeting today, as well as food for Peter and Acol.

9:45 a.m.: Richard leaves and Peter asks us for a ride into town.

10:15 a.m.: We eat breakfast quickly as James is very prompt and we are late.

11:00 a.m.: Drop Peter in town and pick up James. He has been waiting for a while. In addition, there is a third man he wants to introduce to the work. He is a math teacher and wants to write math books for the school children in Cøllø.

11:30 a.m.: We get to Amos' house. Janice goes over the pre-primer and the primer, which need corrections. We discuss the changes. Then we tried out a new game that we devised because of our "Boggling." We put out squares of cards with letters on them. The only letters available are the ones taught in the first seven lessons of the primer. The three men make words using only those letters. I write them down along with their English meaning. After two hours, we had two pages of words to use in those first seven lessons. They enjoyed the game.

2:00 p.m.: I go over the spelling questions I have for the book of twenty stories James wrote and that is nearly ready for publication. As this book will be the basis for the dictionary, we need to spell the words consistently. While working on this, the men eat the sandwiches we brought.

3:00 p.m.: We are exhausted and depart for home.

4:00 p.m.: We eat lunch and I fill the solar shower with water and put it on the porch in the sun. It is too late in the afternoon for it to get hot, but it will warm up enough in an hour to have a comfortable shower. After all, it is still winter!

Love,

L

Dear Harriet,

The "powers that be" appointed James to become a judge at the end of March. He had a law degree and passed the bar, but had never practiced as a lawyer. He had to do two months of military service and then train on how to be a judge. This is a real "brig" to "bench" story. He wouldn't be able to work with us anymore. We appreciate his gifts, abilities, and advice. We are forever grateful for what he's given to the program.

There are a couple of men who may replace him. To produce more books for new readers, we needed more writers. So, we scheduled a writer's workshop. We had six Cølløs and one Ndogo man attending. In the Alphabet Storybook, we have a picture and a word at the top of the page and then two others lower down. We wanted stories about the top picture, so if it was *A a agag* "crow" then we wanted a story about a crow. The next picture was *Ä ä äl* "plow." The mistake I made in choosing the top picture, which no one corrected, was the word for *T t tulø* "owl." Cølløs are very uncomfortable with owls as they associate them with death.

James was going to teach at the writer's workshop, but I had to do it along with my colleagues. We met 9:00 to 1:00 in a house that had no power from 7:00 to 3:00. It made me grateful for the dust storm that brought the temperature into the 80s.

The men needed practice using the spelling rules and getting used to other people checking their work. Janice, John, Pam, and Wanda helped with teaching as I had never seen a workshop. This was the first of what became the Khartoum Workshop Programme.

On the last day of the course, James showed up at our house at 7:15. Janice was in the shower and I was still in my nightgown, which looked like a sleeveless dress. Many ladies wear night-dresses around the house during the day. James had giardia and needed medicine. He brought a friend, a Muslim Cøllø with an MA in linguistics who wanted to talk shop some time. We got them out of the house by 8:15 so we could prepare for the day.

Once we arrived, we had a closing ceremony where we gave out certificates. After breakfast, we loaded up and headed to St. Joseph Press. They had agreed to give us a tour and demonstrate the equipment. They had prepared well for our visit, showing us how the computers worked and how to make negative plates. The process for making a book included printing, binding, trimming, and even using slugs for typesetting. It took two hours, and we learned a great deal.

Love,

L

Dear Harriet,

While the electricity was on consistently in Mogran, during March, it was off in most of the city from 7:00 to 4:00. So, if we needed to do any photocopying, we had to be at the office after 4:00. We wanted to make a final copy of James' book to send to the printer in Nairobi. We arrived at 4:15, but the computer acted up, then the printer didn't work, and it took until 9:00 p.m. to get it started. We planned to sleep at Manshia, so we worked until 1:00 a.m. After two more evenings, we finished the photocopying and sent it off to Nairobi.

On one of those evenings, we quit at 8:30 and joined Russ and Lynda for a cup of tea and a chat. We left at 9:15, only to have one of our tires disintegrate fifty yards from the gate. The tread came off, leaving the steel belts sticking out like the fur on a frightened cat. Russ changed it for us. Those tires had 50,000 miles on bad roads, so we got our money's worth. We are now trying to buy new ones. It isn't easy.

We looked for tires for the car. There's no choice of brand, and we will have to pay at least $150 each. We had another flat, a nail, and were grateful to have a spare tire to use. Our Cøllø friend, Kent, helped us look, as he could get a better price than we could. He found a "new" tire that had been buried in the ground for a year. Then they offered him a "new" tire, only slightly used.

We were grateful the government lifted the import restrictions on tires. We purchased new ones! They cost $431 each.

A friend of ours wanted to buy a new Toyota pickup. On Thursday, the cost was £s1,400,000 ($113,822). By Saturday, the price had increased to £s1,430,000 ($116,260). Inflation is no joke here!

Love,

L

Dear Harriet,

The weather in Khartoum is a frequent topic of conversation. There is more to it than hot and hotter. There is also the hottest. It is dry and chilly from mid-November to (hopefully late) March. The air gets so dry that the Sudanese rub Vaseline into the cracks on their feet. I used lots of cream on mine as well. Then in April it turns humid and hot, over 100°F during the day. April marks the beginning of the dust storm season. As the heat intensifies, the demand for electricity to run air conditioners, air coolers, fans, refrigerators, and freezers increases. Everyone wants a cold drink and a cool place to sit. Temperatures vary between 90°F (33°C) and 120°F (50°C) from April through the middle of November. The humidity fluctuates between 50% to 100% for the same period. At night, temperatures only cool down 10°-20°F, so we get little relief.

The rains come during July, August, and September, with occasional showers in October. During that time, the Blue Nile rises twenty feet as water flows from the highlands of Ethiopia. In 1966, the government built a hydroelectric dam near Damazine for irrigation and electricity. The power generated by the turbines during August and September should have solved the chronic shortage of electricity in the capital. But such was not the case.

One summer we were suffering through multiple power shortages and wondering why the dam at Damazine was not helping us more. Then we heard a report that engineers had gone to Damazine to investigate. The current brought water and rubbish to the dam: trees, rocks, and branches. Several of the screens designed to catch this debris had broken and needed replacing. Most significantly, a large boat had sunk right in front of the intake valves for the turbines. The boat needed to go.

The engineers returned to Khartoum and got word to various embassies that if they removed the boat, the power supply would improve. Several embassies and larger companies contributed to a fund to get the boat out of the river. A significant amount of money was required, but eventually, they raised the full amount. The representative then approached the officials and asked them to take care of the situation. The officials took the money. Their reported response was to hire a local *fakii* (a person consulted for a cure using the Koran and/or magic and charms). He put an enchantment on the boat, but it didn't move. They had paid the money in advance, so you can be sure that, unlike the boat, it was gone. The problems of electricity continued for the rest of the summer.

You may be wondering why I told you this story. I believe that, if it is true, the authorities had the resources available to remove the boat. But there is a mixture of the ancient in modern Sudanese life. They have technology and the ability to use it. For reasons we can't understand, they don't choose that option, but return to the old ways. To the western mind, this choice is incomprehensible. Somehow, to the Sudanese mind, it is logical.

Love,

L

Dear Harriet,

Early May brought temperatures of 120°F (50°C) in the shade. When we entered the house, we marveled at how cool it was at 104°F. Even the Sudanese were complaining about the heat.

We decided to train Mary as she supposedly knew how to type, but it was a unique style of one finger using alternate hands, regardless of where the letters were. One hand rests, the other types a letter, then it rests while the other has a go. I picked up a computer typing program in the UK. It teaches touch typing and starts with the letters f-j. Mary had to match it with no mistakes before continuing. She got to the second set of letters after 1.5 hours! I could see this would be a slow process! She is a widow with three children and not much income. We are paying her travel money plus a small salary while she trains. Once she can type, we'll pay her more. My backlog of keyboarding is getting greater by the day. After ten hours, she was still on Lesson 1. The program rang a bell when she got something wrong, and I think she liked to hear it ring.

We sent fifty transition books and 150 copies of all Cøllø books, along with two teachers, to Renk, south of Khartoum and north of Malakal. There is great interest in learning to read. We can't go because of the war in the south, but the work is spreading. Classes are in progress across the city and we are racing to get the primer lessons done and tested! We need a full-time photocopy person.

Love,

L

Dear Harriet,

The longer we are in Sudan, the more insane it becomes. In the middle of May, the government decided to change the currency notes. You give them old bills; they give you new ones with a different color. The black market rate was £s80/$1.00, while the official exchange rate was £s12/$1. We shopped for vegetables, fruit, ground beef, cleaning materials, milk, cheese, and eggs, spending £s3,200. We needed identity cards before changing money at the bank, and we had waited for months to get them.

They began giving out the new currency on a Sunday. Everyone must change their bills within one week by the 18th of May. At first, you took your money in and they gave you up to £s5,000. They opened an account and deposited the remainder of your funds there. One of our friends runs a large organization and they need £s300,000 to pay salaries. He could only get £s5,000 this week and they'll decide later about the rest. Another source said they were running low on the new notes. They take your cash and give you a receipt. You can't spend that in the market. No one would EVER take a check!

No one believed the money deposited in the bank would return to its rightful owner. So, Janice and I stopped in a shop and purchased a couple of dresses. Then, we ordered gold necklaces with our names in Arabic. We asked if we could pay in old currency. The owner agreed, then he said, "If you have any left over, feed it to the goats. At least you can get the milk." He also made this prediction:

"Ah, you people who have been here during this time. After you die, St. Peter will meet you at the gate (of heaven). When he sees you were in Khartoum during these days, he will say, 'I have no more questions. Go on in!'"

Many of our Sudanese friends changed what little money they had, so we asked them to change a bit for us. Another expat friend had made the exchange, but was leaving the country for a holiday. She sold us her cash. On the last Saturday, we had the documents we needed. We hurried to the bank early and joined a hundred others sitting on mats on the ground. It took several hours, but we received cash in the end.

Love,

L

Dear Harriet,

People told us various rationales for this frustrating decision. (1) All the merchants kept their cash at home, not in the bank; so, the banks didn't have any and this was a way to recover it. (2) The political parties had most of the currency, and the government wanted it. (3) The government wanted to control inflation and bring down prices. So, they were limiting the amount of money available. If people spend less, merchants must charge less, and heaven is on the way. The only catch was they couldn't reduce the supply of money since no one gave them any, so they took it by force.

No one knew what was going on or why, but everyone felt it was stressful. If this didn't bring down the government, I didn't know what would. It didn't.

We heard interesting stories during this time. One very wealthy man had stored his money in a safe room at his home. After this decree, he took a truckload of money to the bank. The bank took his money and gave him a bit of cash and a receipt. The old man suffered a severe shock and died right there from a heart attack.

It was time for Eid al Dahia (Feast of Sacrifice), so many people were buying sheep. One man tried to pay for his sheep with a check. This did not satisfy the owner, and when the man tried to take the sheep away, the owner pulled out a knife and stabbed him.

Our travel agent told us that to pay for a ticket, he had to have double the amount of the ticket in his bank account. Otherwise, the bank would not honor the check and the receiver wouldn't accept it. So, how do I know how much money you have in your account? I wouldn't take a check either!

We heard that the government had ordered the new bills from Japan. After the first container of money arrived, the money change happened. They ran out of cash to give back to people. Of course, the Japanese wanted payment, but someone said the Sudan government didn't have money to pay. So, instead, they placed an order in Britain. Again, the first shipment arrived and Sudan defaulted. As a result, the money had slightly different markings, and people were asking if they were counterfeit. The bank took everything, so maybe what they said is true.

If you have any old currency after 10:00 a.m. Saturday, feed it to a goat.

Love,

L

Dear Harriet,

Nile Safari was a private company that flew small planes in Sudan. If a few people needed to go somewhere, chartering a Nile Safari plane was a good choice. A group of Presbyterian pastors chartered one of them to fly to their annual conference in Malakal. While there, the army hired the same company to bring soldiers back to Khartoum. On the return journey, the SPLA shot down the plane. No survivors. The pilot was British.

After this event, people checked if the plane would still bring the pastors back. No. Nile Safari refused to fly to the south. The pastors had to get back as best they could.

Perhaps the intense heat is contributing to the craziness. Janice checked the temperature, and it was 130°F in the shade! It rained twice so the humidity is high and no one feels like doing anything.

Dust storms are a weekly, if not daily, occurrence. It's time for a vacation.

The government signed an agreement allowing Lifeline Sudan to bring food to the country. They can go overland to the north and west, but rains have come to the south and roads are impassable. The only way to get food to the most needy southern areas is by Hercules cargo planes. The West won't use planes because they disapprove of the government. So, the people there will starve. It makes me angry and bitter because I suspect the timing was no accident.

Over several months, SIL sent $26,000 worth of aid into Sudan. Part of it went via Zaire into southern Sudan. The rest reached a church in Khartoum and kept more than one hundred families from starving. Several reliable churches in Juba distributed forty-five tons of grain, fifteen tons of beans, and two hundred gallons of cooking oil.

The Chattanooga Times published the following in April 1991:

> *"Famine has reached crisis proportions in Sudan where up to 11 million people face severe hunger and hundreds of thousands may die, US officials said Thursday. Sudan is the worst off of six African nations experiencing severe food shortages, the official said. All told, between 33 million and 35 million Africans are at risk in Sudan, Mozambique, Angola, Liberia, Ethiopia and Somalia... the infant mortality rate is 100 percent in some Sudanese villages."*

The Bible says, "Love your enemies and pray for those who misuse and abuse you." (Luke 6:27-28.) I never felt I had enemies before, but now I do. And loving and praying are far from what I want to do for them.

Love,

L

Dear Harriet,

As we prepared for a three-week vacation in Egypt, we got our Egyptian visas, the Sudanese exit/reentry visas and a booking on Air France. Janice went to get traveler's checks from the bank. When they learned she was going to Egypt, they gave her a letter of credit to their branch in Cairo. She also wanted $50 in cash, but they didn't want to give that to her. Getting angry would not help, so she explained, "I know this isn't your fault, but how will I get from the airport into Cairo?"

"Your friend can pick you up."

"But my friend is working and may not be available. Then what will I do?"

Eventually, he gave her the $50. That was the maximum amount of US dollars we could take out of the country.

We lived off what we had and hoped for better times. We planned to stock up in Egypt.

James asked us to buy him a suit for his new job as a judge. Upon arrival, we met a few of the thirty-nine Cølløs in Cairo who had gone through the transition book. They were eager to meet us. We gave them their certificates of completion, and asked them to help find James' suit.

They took us to a tailor and explained what we needed. The suit had to have a waistcoat. That idea never crossed our minds. We found a nice shirt and wanted to get a tie to go with it. We chose a nice red one to match one stripe in the shirt. Oh no! A red tie signaled one was a communist and would frighten the defendant. So, we chose a different color.

The tailor worked on the suit while we were in Alexandria. Upon our return, we picked it up. It was beautifully done. (I give more details of our adventures in Egypt in another book in this series.)

As we prepared to depart, the Cølløs came to greet us and asked to see James' suit. We brought it out. They opened the coat to make sure the waistcoat was there. As soon as they saw it, they said, "Ah, the judge!"

James in his suit

We sold them the books we had, but that was not enough. Once back in Khartoum, we sent more. It was encouraging to see their enthusiasm.

Love,

L

Dear Harriet,

We knew we were back in Sudan after our vacation when we had one expatriate and eight Sudanese visitors, plus Acol. The next day, we had five guests for lunch, which meant I spent much of the day cooking and entertaining. I sat down at my computer at 7:30.

The Cølløs got hold of a copy of *The Jungle Doctor* books and asked if they could translate them. We wrote to the appropriate people and received permission. Once they translated it, I input the text and corrected the spelling. After printing it out, the teachers went over it and made more corrections. I did it in three parts. By mid-July, part 1 was on its fifth revision, part 2 on its third, and part 3 on its second revision.

Our water supply proved inconsistent. When we had water, it came as a muddy trickle. The water going into our filter was chocolate colored. It improved one day, so we did the laundry. In Fitihab, where Pastor Peter and Rachel lived, they didn't have water for six days. We mustn't complain. We kept two barrels that we refilled when the water was on. One air cooler is low enough to pour in a bucket of water. The other cooler is over a door, so not as accessible.

Our neighbor Chris bought a microwave, and we had access to it. With this addition, we could cook with the solar cooker, the gas stove/oven, an electric toaster oven, or the microwave! It's always good to have multiple alternatives.

Many long-term residents of Sudan decided it was time to move. We had developed a friendship with William and Henrietta, a Syrian-Sudanese couple. Henrietta knew Khartoum very well and often told us where to buy things. They decided to move to the US to be with their son, so they sold off their furnishings. We bought a set of living room furniture, two sofas, and three chairs with wooden frames and cotton cushions. We also purchased two writing desks, three lamps, a small dining table and an old television and video player. These items provided much needed comfort. The only incentive for me to take time off and relax was to have some light entertainment available. Janice's family can send video cassettes, and we have a friend with an American VCR.

My parents sent desperately needed money for the Cøllø teachers. The government didn't pay primary school teachers for three months, and they were in dire straits. They were thrilled to get this help, as a "gift from America."

When the organization using our outside office left the country, we gained added space for the Cøllø work. We found a large desk and an enclosed cupboard for the new office.

Typing was not Mary's gift, so we let her go. Then we hired Roda, who had experience with a manual typewriter. She has seven children and her husband, a doctor, was in prison for fifteen months with no charges ever brought against him.

Love,

L

Dear Harriet,

When James became a judge and no longer had time to work with us, the Cøllø Language Oversight Committee appointed a replacement, Nyikwec. His name means Leopard. The committee instructed us and the teachers that no one would receive a salary. Nyikwec works with us and supervises the classes in and around Khartoum. He receives incentive pay for his help along with his regular government teacher's salary. The elders knew if Janice and I paid salaries, it would create dependency. Instead, we used money from the sale of books to provide incentive pay. One flaw in that plan is that Cølløs can't say "no." If a friend asks for a book, but wants to pay later, they must give the book to him. "Later" never comes for getting paid.

Janice got a new computer and after much struggle, sweat and tears, learned to use it. She began creating the primer. How do you do that?

Janice working on the primer

First, Janice discussed what content she needed to include with me and our literacy consultants. Then we decided in what order to teach things. Next, Janice asks Nyikwec to make up stories, sentences, comprehension questions, lists of words, etc. She takes that information and puts the lesson together. She and Nyikwec go over it and make changes. I stick my nose in to see what they are up to and make further suggestions. When the lesson is ready, an older teacher checks it for accuracy and clarity to make sure it teaches GOOD Cøllø.

Once the lessons have passed these tests, they are ready to go onto the computer, and be printed out, photocopied, and given to the teachers to try out with one or two students. They come back with suggestions about what works. They revise the lessons and try them out again. It is not a simple task, but what a joy to see people learning to read. Their enthusiasm makes the effort worthwhile.

One of my goals for August was to get two books and the 1992 calendar ready for the printer. Without the help of our five teachers, it would be impossible. They are taking on more and more of the responsibility and doing a good job.

Love,

L

Dear Harriet,

One goal SIL had in Sudan was to facilitate Bible translation. The Cølløs had a 1977 New Testament that they couldn't read. Even the translators couldn't read it accurately. Only a few people read it and most seem untouched by it.

Pastor Samuel, along with the Cøllø Language Oversight Committee, wanted to see the translation restarted. The Bible Society of Sudan had overseen the original translation with the Presbyterian Church. But, the Catholic Church used a different translation with different letters and spelling. SIL and the Sudan Bible Society agreed to work together to re-translate the Cøllø New Testament and add the Old Testament. Both organizations saw the importance of churches working together. Now that the Cølløs had agreed on a new writing system, they wanted to use it in the translation. The Bible Society of Sudan took responsibility for the translation with the lead translator, Otto, a Catholic.

We trust the new spelling system and revising the content will impact hearts and lives.

Love,

L

Dear Harriet,

Fuel rationing remained a constant in our lives. Siphoning petrol became a national pastime. Before arriving in Sudan, the only thing I knew about siphoning fuel was not to suck on the hose. It was dangerous and unpleasant to get gasoline in your mouth. But, while sitting in the petrol queue, we saw a lot of siphoning. The driver inserted a piece of garden hose into the fuel tank and sucked on the other end. Once the flow started, he put his end of the hose into a jerry can.

The maximum amount of fuel per week was six gallons. You needed to drain the tank to make sure you had enough room. "Why?" you ask. Petrol was only dispensed into a vehicle with a license plate. If you couldn't get your full allotment into the tank, the attendant would not put the rest into a jerry can. "Why?" Because it didn't have a license plate. But one could pull away from the pump to siphon the fuel out of the tank. Then, the attendant put the rest of the ration in the tank. Sudanese are sticklers for rules, and the challenge was to get around them.

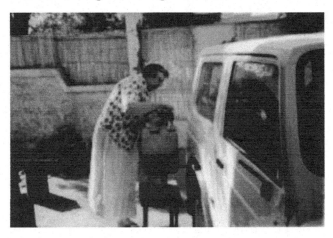

Janice with fuel for the car. (Credit: Kathy Smith)

Some drivers had no working fuel gauge, so they put a jerry can on the hood or dashboard with a hose leading to the engine. That way, they knew how much fuel was available. Since that functioned as the gas tank, the attendants would fill the jerry can.

Motorcycles went to the station twice a week to get two gallons at a time. One of our employees' bikes required gasoline and oil to be mixed before putting it into the tank. The rationing system did not allow for that. Richard had the jerry can on the back of this bike to get the fuel ration. They refused. He returned to the office and attached a small hose from the jerry can to the engine. It did nothing. But at the station, he convinced the attendant the tube fueled the engine. Since the jerry can was now the tank, he had no trouble getting his fuel.

Fuel pumps run on electricity. One day, I reached the pump after my three-hour wait to find the electricity had gone off. I had to wait for the generator to start. But sometimes the generator was broken, and we had to wait for someone to repair it before the fueling resumed. I faced the decision: Should I risk leaving, later to find there was no more fuel, or should I sit and wait for what could be hours? It was not a straightforward decision. Either way, the result was costly.

Love,

L

Dear Harriet,

Visiting was a very important social event in Sudan. Life in a community meant that people needed to stay in touch with their neighbors and their relatives. There was a high expectation to visit co-workers, even after spending the entire week working with them.

I suspect women visited each other during the late morning hours after breakfast and before lunch preparation started. However, our household worked most of the day, so visiting happened in the afternoons. When a household expected visitors, they left the gate to the street ajar. Anyone, and I mean anyone, could walk to the gate, tap on it and step into the compound. One of the children welcomed the visitor. Women visited behind the house, in a secluded part of the yard. The men gathered in the front near the gate.

Once the heat of the day had passed, the furniture moving began. They moved beds outside, as well as a few chairs and small tea tables. Everything had its place in the shade. Then the women chatted with anyone who turned up. As each visitor arrived, the hostess greeted the person. Some women got a handshake, but a good friend got hugs and kisses on the cheek. Once the guest sat down, the hostess summoned a young girl to bring a glass of water. In a bit, either juice or Pepsi appeared and, if one stayed longer, hot tea. If I tried to leave early, the hostess insisted I stay because "*shay jaaya!*" (tea is coming).

I learned not to empty my glass unless I wanted more. Leaving a little water or tea or soda in the glass signaled you had drunk enough. If someone came in and drained the glass of water, one of the girls standing by refilled it. The women sipped their drinks while imparting the gossip they had collected and discovering what the host family had heard.

Once they had discussed the price for meat, a bed sheet, or the new linoleum on the floor, they took their leave. Or, they turned to discover how much Arabic I might know. Once they realized I could understand their questions, I was in for a grilling. Before the visit, I practiced a few entertaining stories about the market or my family to contribute to the afternoon's entertainment. My problem became getting home again. They wanted me to stay, as I had many new things to say. They would discuss my stories and my visit throughout the neighborhood for weeks. I love to be the center of attention, and that was my opportunity! By the end of an hour, I felt exhausted and full of sweet drinks.

No topic was taboo on these afternoon visits. They asked how much we paid for rent on the house. I had to be careful about that one, as foreigners paid more than locals. I decided to answer what was asked: "How much rent do you pay?" So, I told them what my portion was. I did not mention two or three others paid the same amount. They asked about the price of my car, the chairs I bought, and the food I purchased. They wanted to make sure sellers didn't cheat me by telling me what I should pay. Of course, I could ask them the same questions.

I loved to inquire about their cultural activities. They thought it was so funny that I didn't know. The younger children sat near their mother with eyes wide, taking in the amusing things this white person said. They overlooked my grammatical mistakes, and I learned to throw in the odd English word when I couldn't remember the correct Arabic term. They seemed able to guess, or some "secret" English student supplied the needed word, revealing her abilities.

I assume that visits with men were similar, but inclined to politics. Sometimes the head of the household came to the women's quarters to greet me and have a chat. The men often spoke English and liked the chance to practice. The women fell silent while he was there, and his presence put a bit of a damper on the occasion.

Other women got in and out in ten to fifteen minutes. I guess they visited more often, and so had less to catch up on or share. Many women made the rounds each evening. I rarely turned up, so it was hard to leave anywhere in under an hour, because they would show me the full range of hospitality.

As I exited their gate, the street activity hit me. Nightlife seemed like a party. It was a relief to enter my quiet, enclosed world, where English was the predominant language. If I had it to do over, I would visit more and work less.

Love,

L

Dear Harriet,

In October, All Souls church in London again gave me a special gift of money to pass along to those in need. Prices increased five times in a few weeks, and everyone I knew was struggling. Sudan experienced a drought and resulting famine. For months afterwards, we bought sacks of grain and delivered them to the homes of those in need.

My parents celebrated their fiftieth wedding anniversary on October 18, 1991. I traveled home to celebrate this special time. I returned home more often to check on my parents. These visits were brief, as I didn't want to leave Janice on her own for too long. It was a balancing act.

Frances and J.T.'s 50th anniversary dinner

My dear friend, Sr. Theresa Nyathow, wrote to my parents. She wished them a Happy Christmas, prosperous New Year 1992, and belated congratulations for the fiftieth wedding anniversary. She continued, "I hope you are keeping well and still very much interested in the mission of your daughter. God bless you for always being the support to Leoma in that mission and service to the Cøllø people. She is doing great things. Pray for our nation and us that things might improve. It is faith in God that keeps us going. Pray that our faith may stay strong and genuine to what we believe."

I returned to Khartoum from the US on December 10 with lots of overweight luggage! Janice and I didn't have a handover because Janice's father had died while on vacation in Australia! She immediately left for England and didn't return as planned because her mother needed her. Wanda stayed with me and that was a tremendous help.

My Cøllø friends came to greet me. First, they wanted to make sure I knew about Janice's father. Then they asked about my parents. I had fourteen visitors in one day.

The Sudanese fear the cold, so when it cools off in mid-November, they ask for blankets. By mid-December, it got down to 48°F at night. Many people get sick and even die from the change of temperature.

The teachers and I worked hard to make a song sheet of Christmas songs. We were ready for the big day with song sheets and 1992 calendars!

Just before Christmas, the army surrounded an area where 100,000 people lived. These people had purchased land and built houses. But the government decided they didn't want them there, so they turned up with bulldozers. They knocked down the houses and burned them. When they met with resistance, they shot into the crowd. We heard over fifty people died. One of our teachers, Peter M, lost his home because the government decided to build a new road there. He came to share our garage with the Anyua guard. While this was a relief for him, he turned out to be a gift to us.

Love,

L

Chapter 5:
1992

Dear Harriet,

In January, we met for our biennial conference in Limuru, Kenya, high in the mountains among the tea plantations. So, the weather was lovely, food was available, and the tensions of the Gulf War were far away. Once our meetings concluded, however, we had to face reality once again.

Russ was the local director of Khartoum, so he returned first to assess the situation. If things were problematic, he planned to collect valuables, including my computer, and bring them to Kenya. If safe, he would give the go-ahead for his family and me to return. We shopped for those last-minute things: car parts, dried vegetables, cornmeal, rice, tea, coffee, cheese... Finally, we heard "Come ahead."

We hurried on with the long list of things we needed to do. I took most of the Cøllø materials that had been printed in Kenya. Then, if I had to leave, the team could distribute those materials. Friends packed the books for me.

At 5:10 (ten minutes after office closing time), I realized my ticket was still at the travel agent's office. Our flight was to leave at 8:00 the next morning. Dan, our Nairobi Office Manager, rushed into town on his motorbike to catch someone in the office and get the ticket. After two trips and lots of stress, he retrieved the ticket at 7:00 p.m.

We packed into the wee hours of the morning, arriving at the airport at 6:00 a.m. with over 800 pounds of luggage, mostly books. The officials gave us a generous discount on the overweight. We paid half, and the three of us and seventeen pieces of luggage headed to the plane.

Once we arrived in Khartoum, I found the house in good order, the cats healthy, and money was more available.

While it was summer in Kenya, Khartoum had winter. Temperatures plummeted to 42°F. I thought of buying a heater! No one remembered it ever being that cold. Instead, I wore my heavy sweater continually until I got under my blankets in bed. Wearing long sleeves reminded me how dirty everything is. I have a terminal case of "ring around the cuff" to add to the regular collar problem.

Janice has decided to work in Khartoum for four months and then go home for two. I'm not sure how long she can keep that up. As a group, we were consulting with thirty-one languages. It overwhelmed us to think of the potential impact on the country if these languages developed as they should. That thought inspired me to take a nap to prepare for the upcoming workshop.

Love,

L

Dear Harriet,

We regularly spent time at the market since we liked to eat. Markets like the one near our house were small. If we wanted the full range of produce, we had to go to one of the large markets. A Sudanese market is most like the Farmer's Market at home or the produce section of the grocery store enlarged and out of doors.

The three largest markets were in the middle of Khartoum near the central bus station, in North Khartoum (also called Bahri), and the largest of all was in Omdurman. The Omdurman market stretches over a couple of square kilometers, maybe more. It was the first market I went to in 1982, and the one I knew best. I've never seen all of it. The central market in Khartoum, alas, is no more. The government decided they didn't want people gathering in the center of town as it might lead to disorder. I think a wealthy Arab wanted to build on this prime real estate. After its closure, merchants purchased Toyota pickups and sold their food on the side of the road.

They divide the markets into different sections: vegetables, fruit, meat, bread, spices; dried goods such as beans, lentils, dried tomatoes; perfumes and incense; and cloth. In the household goods section, one could pick up a water filter, buckets, hoses, charcoal stoves, rope, cord, flashlights, basins, knives, silverware, and dishes. Another area specializes in plumbing and other larger household building needs. There are a few bookshops and clothing stores.

Sun-dried tomatoes for sale in Omdurman market

My favorite shop in the Omdurman market was a street over from Gold Street. The owner, a deaf-mute, sold camel saddles, camel hair rugs, whips, mattresses, blankets, pillows, and chair cushions. One of his sons interpreted, signing to him what we wanted and negotiating the price. He was a very savvy businessman.

Nearby was the famous Omdurman bead market. The sellers only came on Friday and Tuesday. The array of beads was amazing. I found it hard to buy anything because there was too much choice. They offered valuable amber, if you got the real one. The trick was identifying the real from the fakes. One could find valuable antique beads if you knew what to look for. I never knew those things, and worrying about it just spoiled the experience. So, I chose what I liked, tried to buy it for a good price, and then enjoyed it. Talking with the salesmen was more fun than shopping, but then I'm not a shopper.

One of the many traders offering his beads for sale

Gold Street offers what its name implies: gold. Sudan has mines with high quality eighteen karat gold. Much of the jewelry was crafted in the Gulf. They have beautiful filigree work in necklaces and the special headdresses women wear at their weddings, along with beautifully designed rings and bracelets, all sold by weight.

The shops looked shabby and none too secure. I assume each shop came equipped with a sturdy safe.

In the Bahri market, the street boys drove me nuts. They hung around the cars and pestered me to let them guard the car or carry my basket. I learned to have one of them wash the car, and thus guard it. I hired another boy to carry my large *guffa* or shopping basket. He not only carried the increasingly heavy basket, but fended off the others, so I could get on with my shopping in relative peace. Also, the basket-boy alerted me to inflated prices. The vegetable and fruit section of this market was under one large roof. Each seller had a small space to display his produce. I preferred to buy several things at one stall and then move on to another. In that way, I had a better chance of spotting a rare treat such as celery. Whenever I buy a big stalk of celery in the USA, I remember the small, straw-sized drooping strands that passed for celery in Sudan. It was just too hot for that crop to grow. But when added to a stew or a salad, we could taste it, and it was a delightful addition.

The butcher was my least favorite section. They didn't slaughter on Tuesday or Friday, so only leftover meat was available on Wednesdays and Saturdays. I identified which shop to go to by the size of the leg or side of meat hanging on a large hook just outside the window. The flies were the first visitors. When I looked interested, the butcher came out with his blood-stained apron, knife in hand. If I wanted meat with bones, as most Sudanese do, then he got out his small machete. Sudanese flavor their stews with a little meat and the marrow from the bone that the butcher hacks into small pieces. One should chew carefully on pieces of meat, as the bone shards are sharp. Foreigners preferred cuts of filet, tenderloin, or rump roast. They sold tenderloin by the piece and roast by the kilo. They unceremoniously dumped the lump of meat onto one side of the balance scales and placed the weights on the other side. If the meat was less than the requested amount, the butcher would whack off another piece or two to make up the proper weight. I tried to get them to cut off the skin and excess fat, at least after they weighed it. They worked with knives so sharp I would likely cut off my hand. Hard experience taught me cutting away gristle and fat dulled my knives in a short time!

The author poses with the butcher and the fruit vendor in front of the rack of meat

When possible, I used the same shops or vendors. If they knew me, then I didn't have to go through the hassle of bargaining as long or as hard. They considered me their *zabuuna* or regular customer and the relationship became the most important part of the transaction. If there were a shortage of eggs, they might let me have some of their secret stash. It's another lesson in what it means to be part of a community.

Love,

L

Dear Harriet,

Winter is a great time for vegetables. We have green beans, cauli-flower, peas, and maybe celery! I learned to blanch and freeze these, so we had variety to enjoy the rest of the year. We also have visitors in the winter. The secretary from Nairobi paid us a visit and trained Roda. Arabic doesn't use punctuation, so she needs help with that. She's learning to use my computer so she can input materials, and I will get on with my list.

Roda's husband was released from prison after twenty-one months. The authorities never brought any charges against him. He can't leave the city or be in a government position but may resume his medical practice. If he works, they can move to a better place with electricity and running water.

Acol likes to be alone in the house one day a week to clean unhindered. The rest of the week she cooks, irons, washes mounds of dishes, and tidies up stuff. She will need to get going in Janice's room as it is inches thick in dust. I plan to buy new mattresses on Friday as the ones we've been using are hard and flat.

Love,

L

Dear Harriet,

A friend of mine named John had an adventure while visiting the north of Sudan. He shared this story with me. I am including it with his permission.

John visited a village that operated a joint bus service with three neighboring villages. Prospective travelers purchased a ticket from one of the designated shops. Each shop should only sell ten seats. There were no printed tickets; it was by word of mouth. Once a week the forty-seater bus traveled from these villages to the capital.

Early in the morning, he stood at the departure point along with seventy-nine other passengers and one sheep. There was agitation amongst the prospective passengers, as they realized each shopkeeper had sold far more than their allotted ten tickets. John understood what had happened. Everyone in the village was related to one of the shopkeepers, and, as a relative, he could not tell the purchaser, "Sorry, the bus is already full."

John wondered how they could resolve this problem. A villager assured him that everyone would get on board and, when they encountered a police checkpoint, the driver would pay the prescribed fine for an overloaded bus.

After a three-hour wait, everyone got on the bus. People sat on boxes of cokes in the gangway and on other people's laps. The narrow seat in front of John, designed for three, had five. One man had even squashed himself between the driver and the driver's door. The remaining travelers piled onto the roof along with the excess of luggage.

After everyone was on board, they decided there was room inside for the sheep. Somehow, the bus moved, but felt like a swaying ship. The driver used extreme care so no one fell from the roof and to prevent the whole bus turning over. Slowly, the bus traveled up and down the many sand dunes. John wondered how the roof could withstand such a load, but it did. With the heat of so many bodies crammed together, it was impossible to escape the smell of humanity, and don't forget the sheep! Despite the dangers and long, long hours, I'm pleased to say John made it safely back to Khartoum.

Love,

L

Dear Harriet,

What is the national flower and national bird of Sudan? The answer, according to my friend Lois, is "the plastic bag." The bird is the white-breasted Sudanese *kiis*, otherwise known as the "bag-bird."

Plastic bags were the most ubiquitous item in Sudan except for the dust. They imported millions and millions of them from China and used them in markets throughout the country. The bags were lightweight, rarely reused, and so flew away once they were empty. Any gust of wind caught the bags and transported them until they caught on a devil's apple bush or a barbed-wire fence. The bush thrived in the hot, dry soil in the north. Goats wouldn't eat these poisonous plants. So, they collected dust and bloomed plastic bags.

Then there were the bag farms. Any barbed-wire fence could serve as a breeding ground for a bag farm. The bags blew around until they caught on the barbs, where they appeared to multiply. If there were enough fences, they might create a bag plantation.

There was talk of using bags that disintegrated in the sun. But we feared that in the intense sun of Sudan, the bags might disintegrate before we got home from the market with our goods.

The streets and gutters filled up with dirty, torn plastic bags. The government thought of ways to prevent this problem. One suggestion was to use heavier bags that did not fly around so easily. Also, if people paid for the bags, they might reuse them.

We tried to get ladies interested in making things out of plastic bags. We suggested they collect used bags, and wash and dry them. Then weave them together to make sleeping mats. We trained one woman how to do this, but when she taught a class, she bought new bags to use, which defeated the purpose. As far as I know, no one has found a good use for the bag flowers or the bag birds.

Love,

L

———

Dear Harriet,

We made one last check of *The Jungle Doctor* book. I listened carefully as a teacher read the text. I listened for the light versus heavy vowels, vowel and consonant length, and checked the punctuation. It took four hours. Afterwards, I drove him home, and that took another hour. I ate breakfast at 9:30 and got lunch at 5:45. I was exhausted. After two years of work, we sent *The Jungle Doctor* book for printing. People were eager to read it and I rejoiced that we finished it.

We had forty-five Sudanese from seventeen languages turn up for the first introduction to translation principles course. Five of them, from two languages, had no writing system. One of those groups, the As, had never tried to write their language. They didn't have letters for all their sounds. The writer's course came after the translation course. Talk about putting the cart before the horse!

Once the writers workshop began, I taught for an hour and a half, three times a week and helped the Cøllø Catholic bishop, who needed to learn the new spelling rules. Besides teaching and assisting the bishop, I worked with the groups beginning to write their languages.

As the February committee meeting approached, Janice returned. They assumed I was going to translate the Bible for them. We had to convince them we had no intention of doing that. The community could put together a team for that work. Also, we had no time.

The committee members needed to set our priorities for the year. I made a list of activities and the steps required to do them. There was so much to do, I couldn't make those choices. They decided we should focus on training, writing the primer, literature development, and the dictionary. All the other things would either not get done or someone else would do them.

Janice brought me a cartoon with Snoopy lying on his doghouse. It said, "Live for today, learn from yesterday, look to tomorrow, rest for this afternoon!"

Love,

L

Dear Harriet,

There was a small restaurant in Omdurman that became a favorite of mine. It was located in a house on a back alleyway. I had to follow someone on my first visit, as I would never have found the place on my own, even with a map. The streets wind, twist, and turn as if planned by a blindfolded toddler. No sign showed there was a restaurant at this establishment, as I doubt they ever registered it as one. In their eyes, we just joined the family for their lunch and helped pay our way at the end.

An Indian family ran this eatery. The mother spoke little, if any, English, but controlled the happenings in the kitchen. Various children had a part in preparing the spices or beans or rice for the meal. Spices lay in the sun, drying. Another person prepared the lentils for the next day. It was a vegetarian household. Reservations had to be made in advance.

While waiting for others to arrive, guests sat in the family's sitting room. They placed chairs around the wall facing the ever-present television. Without electricity, we just had to wait and fan. When everyone arrived, we washed our hands and made our way into the ten-seater dining room. There were two long, narrow tables with chairs down each side. Once seated, the food arrived. There were plenty of *papadams*—crunchy, thin tortillas along with bowls of steaming lentil curry and vegetables spiced with chili, turmeric, cumin, coriander, mustard seeds, fresh ginger, cinnamon bark, cardamom pods, cloves and, of course, garam masala. They prepared food in ways I had never seen before. The various dishes filled the tables. We each received a metal tray to put our food on. I rarely knew what anything was, but it was delicious. If the contents of any dish ran low, the host whisked it away and refilled it. We ate until we felt stuffed while drinking the delicious lassi (a yogurt drink) to wash it down. At the end, the host brought out a big bowl of rice and another large bowl of delicious yogurt. We took the rice and put the yogurt over it as dessert. I had never tried that before, but after the spicy food, it was nice to cool my mouth and my stomach. This wonderful repast cost $2.00-$3.00, so it was a bargain.

Janice and I took our Cøllø friends there to eat to give them a novel experience. Cøllø meals included meat, so we took our cattle-loving friends to this vegetarian restaurant to expose them to something new. Peter M, Onyoti, and Otto joined us at the Indian restaurant. As they studied the food in front of them, their conversation was revealing. "Well, there is no fish, so we could eat that," said one.

"Since there is no beef, we can eat that," said another.

The meat served controlled the vegetables that they ate. Since there was no meat, they weren't sure what they should eat, but in the end, they ate everything. I don't know if they would have gone back, but they enjoyed the experience and learned another way of looking at the world. By taking them, we had as well.

Love,

L

Dear Harriet,

The exchange rate finally moved as the authorities floated the currency. As soon as they announced the policy, the rate went from £s30/$1 to £s90/$1. The shopkeepers were already selling goods at the new rate, so only subsidized prices increased. Salaries rose from £s900/month to £s1500. In US dollar and buying power terms, it decreased from $30/month to $15.

My desk had so many piles that I lost my sunglasses under one of them. I grouped similar things together and covered my bed, the living room and a chair. With company coming, the reordered stacks will end up back on my desk. Perhaps moving them around will help me get organized or lose it. If I leave unpleasant business items piled up long enough, they become irrelevant and I can throw them away. It is called productive procrastination.

We purchased a water heater, and we use it daily! It is much nicer to get into a warm shower after a chilly day. We don't have many cold days, but when we do... During the hot months, we use the water heater for cold water. The water pipes are underground but heat up until it feels close to scalding. So, storing water in the tank kept it cool. What a life!

Love,

L

Dear Harriet,

Esther invited Janice and me to the Women's World Day of Prayer in early March. On our way there, we heard a funny noise coming from the car. People on the street pointed to us and waved. After a kilometer, we stopped on the empty street to have a look. We had a flat tire. We began finding the equipment to change the tire and removing the spare from the back door of the Suzuki. Somehow, Janice lost her balance and started reeling backwards toward a puddle of muddy water. I tried to catch her hand to help her, but couldn't reach her. She regained her balance just as a man walked up and offered to change the tire for us. I expect he thought we were inept and should never have left our home countries. When he finished, he refused payment. We appreciated his help.

The service began at 9:45 with a procession and singing at one of the Coptic churches. We marched around the compound twice, then sat in the sun for the first hour of the program. We found a bit of shade. Then, we moved *en masse* into the sanctuary. By this time, there were 800 women and a few men in a space designed for 500. Chairs got passed through windows, so most ended up sitting. After everyone was in and seated, someone pointed out that each church group should sit together. As the aisles were filled with chairs, it proved difficult to move, but they did. Five congregations took part in the program that comprised speeches, skits, music, Bible reading, and prayer. The amplifiers worked too well and my eardrums nearly burst! I kept my fingers in my ears to protect them. I was amazed to be in this marble building with white-glass chandeliers. Most churches have a much simpler standard. The program ended at 1:20.

Love,

L

Dear Harriet,

As Janice prepared to return to England, we had a typical morning even though there is no such thing as a typical morning in Sudan.

We got up at 7:00 and went through the usual morning rituals: a devotional time, filling the large orange Igloo thermos with ice and cold water, making coffee, filling the hot water thermos, feeding the cats.

8:00-9:30 Janice drove to the travel agent to book her flight to England. I cooked the cats' food, stamped letters to send out with someone traveling, prepared breakfast, and did a few other odds and ends.

9:30–10:00 Breakfast, during which several people arrive:

Nyikwec, our language officer, arrives early.

Acol takes care of the dish washing, ironing, keeping the house clean, and cooking breakfast for whoever comes to work.

Roda, our typist, comes with a relative to collect grain we offered her.

10:00-1:00 Janice works with Nyikwec on the primer when Pam H arrives. She is the Literacy Consultant who helped with the primer while Janice was away. She wants to keep up with what is going on so when Janice leaves, she can continue the work.

I help Roda decide what to do for the day when Nyikwec brings up the Literacy Day. We need to send out ninety invitations to individual Cølløs along with copies of the program to those who will be speaking. The plans are to explain different aspects of the literacy work and teach a demonstration class. Roda will write the names on the invitations and get them ready to send.

Amid a chaotic morning, Mustafa arrives. He is the maintenance supervisor for Unity High School. Our neighbor Chris is the head of the primary section of the school, and she asked him to see about widening our gate. We want to park the cars inside the compound for security, but the gate is not wide enough. Mustafa brought a builder to estimate the cost.

Peter M comes in to check on the Literacy Day plans and to tell us about his transition class.

Pastor Peter arrives to collect the equipment he had left in our office. He invites us for tea at his house next week.

Santino, the artist, shows up. He is doing posters for the Literacy Day and pictures for the Alphabet Storybook.

Everyone departs at 12:30 after their breakfast is served.

1:00-5:30 Acol leaves for home and we are alone. We do more work on our computers, have our lunch and a rest.

6:00-7:00 We go to Duty Free to spend the last of my hard currency before my declaration form expires. There wasn't much to buy, but we spent what I had.

7:30-9:30 We attend a Bible study with a group from the International Church.

10:00 Home and to bed.

Love,

L

———

Dear Harriet,

We visited Pastor Peter's newly established church in Fitihab on Sunday. There were seventy in attendance. He is doing a wonderful job and has started three churches after an evangelistic campaign.

People came faithfully to the transition classes. Sometimes the participants had learned the old spelling system and found it hard to adapt to the new one. Others found it encouraging, especially the youth. One young man reported he had stopped doing church work because he found it so difficult to read the scripture. But with the new one, he could read easily. It just takes time to get used to new things.

The primer class started late, 6:00-6:40 in the dark. The blackboard assigned to the Cøllø class had no light. I don't know how the students saw what the teacher wrote on the board or how to write in their books.

The primer has forty lessons. After teaching them to small groups, we work with the team to revise it. Then they teach one hundred people and revise it again. At that point, we can print 1000 copies.

We planned the Literacy Day on March 14. The committee and the team wanted to explain more about the project and celebrate the progress made thus far. Forty people attended. On the whole, they thought it a success and plans are underway to continue to hold them so Cølløs gain a better understanding of the writing system. This first one started at 9:00 and should have ended at 1:00. However, arguments began. They were shouting at each other and I prayed fervently. The electricity went off and it was hot and people were hungry. So, we ate lunch and everyone calmed down. Apologies were offered. When we resumed, I explained the rationale behind the decisions, and after another one and a half hours, we reached 90% consensus. The meeting ended at 4:00. People feel strongly about how their language looks when written on paper.

Love,

L

———————

Dear Harriet,

After the translation workshop, we started the writer's workshop on March 24 with thirty-five participants. We didn't have enough food, so we ordered more for the future. One man, Clement, came to the workshop uninvited. He was insistent he HAD to attend. He had tried to force his way into the translation workshop and they had locked him outside the door! I have a soft heart, so I let him come, but explained we had no one to work with him. By the end of the day, he asked if he could bring someone with him the next time so they could discuss issues together. I'd never seen people so eager to learn. We ended up with forty-three participants and staff. (Last year we had seven participants.)

I directed a writer's workshop for three weeks. Each participant brought an animal story from their language. We trained them to make their stories more interesting. They learned to edit and critique their own, as well as others' stories. They also worked on the correct spelling and punctuation. These discussions were lively. We invited artists to join for three sessions to discuss what pictures the groups needed for their stories.

At the end of the course, we turned their stories into a book. This required creative photocopying, but we produced a book for each of the five languages represented. When the participants received the finished product, some had tears in their eyes.

I felt much the same when I received the published version of my PhD dissertation. What a joy to hold that in my hands.

Once the workshop finished, we had fourteen more Cølløs to help with the work. Together with the thirty-four students in Egypt, we had a good number of teachers and writers.

I continued working with the A-team. We agreed on letters for their alphabet and especially how to write their nine vowels. After working on a language with one or two syllables, the A-language was a surprise. Their word for "bat" is *ngalabalung* and for "flower" is *rokolyok*. I hope they will be writing stories in a few months. Then they can plan for translation and literacy and how to fund those activities.

The J-team was one man with a primary school education who didn't understand English, so we worked in Arabic. The J-language resembled Cøllø and was harder to figure out. Since Arabic was the medium of instruction in his primary school, writing English letters proved a challenge. I sent him home to practice.

Love,

L

Dear Harriet,

If I'm just a staff member in a workshop, I can sit in the back and half-listen to lectures I've heard before, and even write a few letters. But as the director, I was responsible for food, tea, sugar, transport money, the schedule, staff meetings, setup, and cleanup. It's exhausting. Not long after this experience, I asked, "Why am I doing this? Shouldn't we have a Sudanese person who can do the logistics for us?" Our director saw the sense of that suggestion and we hired Onyoti for that position. He served on the Cøllø

Language Oversight Committee and had been a school supervisor. However, because he was a southerner, they ended his employment. As a result, when we visited him, we discovered he lived in a tent in an empty church compound. He had built a mud kitchen and put up a shelter of reed mats with plastic sheeting to keep out the sun. He lived there with his wife and five children. Most of the time, his family lived in Renk, south of Khartoum. But during the school holidays, they came for a visit. It seemed unfair that someone with his qualifications should be terminated just because of where he was born. Once he had the logistics job, he did it beautifully and instructed us on how to run closing ceremonies more appropriately. He was a much-welcomed blessing. He moved to a proper house and kept his family with him.

By mid-April the temperatures rose to 115°F in the shade during the day for over two weeks. With the air coolers running at full capacity, I could get the house down to 90°-98°F. If the temperature is higher than my body, my brain stops functioning and I have to do something physical that doesn't require thought.

Love,

L

Dear Harriet,

The government removed subsidies and within a day, the price of a small stick of bread went from £s.50 to £s5.00. Fuel prices rose from £s10/gallon to £s110. Salaries doubled but prices increased by 100 percent. People who were struggling are now in serious trouble. Despite the difficulties they face, people come to the course and work hard. I gain more respect for them as the days pass.

I gained a few more languages, so, as the linguistic consultant, I now had six. It's a linguistic paradise, with language groups beating down my door to get help to analyze them. I feel needed, and it gives me the experience I wanted. Now, I must find how to balance my time and energy to cope with my responsibilities.

I came home on Saturday to discover the water people had come by demanding to see our receipt for the water bill. Acol didn't know where we kept that, so they turned off the water. Chris and I showed them the receipt on Sunday morning, and they turned the water back on. At least we were only without it for one night. The rest of the city still had power cuts from 7:00 a.m.–3:00 p.m. daily. We forgot that until we went to visit. Then it was a shock!

Meanwhile, a major UN food depot was attacked. This happened in Baliet, 30 miles from Malakal, a major town on the White Nile where they unload barges carrying relief supplies from Khartoum. The depot contained 1000 tons of emergency food. They had already distributed 13,000 tons in the preceding weeks to 50,000–70,000 displaced people and drought victims in the region. (*News FreePress*, Apr. 12, 1992.)

Love,

L

Dear Harriet,

Cølløs have interesting expressions. See if you can match them with the correct English meanings.

1. His heart is sweet.

2. His throat is swollen.

3. Something is lying on his chest.

4. His head is bad.

5. He has a little thing in his head.

Here are the meanings mixed up.

A. He is angry.

B. He is fed up.

C. He is crazy.

D. He is happy.

E. He is stubborn.

Here's a Dinka riddle: I am made. The one who made me doesn't want me. The one who buys me doesn't want me. Who am I?

Answers: 1D, 2A, 3B, 4E, 5C, a coffin

Love,

L

Dear Harriet,

In April, I learned my father had cancer in his spine. He took chemotherapy treatment, but my parents didn't think I should come home yet. I prepared to go when they needed me. There was no question about my going as I am their only child.

Due to the continued fighting in southern Sudan, thousands of refugees poured into Kenya. This began the story of the Lost Boys, orphans who fled violence after the government forces killed their parents and burned their villages. They walked hundreds of miles to find safety. Many died on the way, but for the ones who made it to Kenya, some were able to relocate to the United States.

I took a vacation in Kenya and attended our entity conference, as well as an anthropology workshop during May and June. A terrible genocide occurred in Rwanda during this time. Friends warned me not to eat Nile Perch. These fish are carnivores and had possibly fed on the bodies of those killed in Rwanda. That news will put you off eating fish!

Part of my vacation consisted of a stay in the Aberdares near Mount Kenya. The lodge was beautiful, with hundreds of flowers and lots of green grass. My *banda* included a sitting room with fireplace and a separate bedroom to myself. I looked at Mount Kenya from the verandah. They provided meals, and I didn't speak to anyone except the staff the entire week. It was a time to pray and think through my growing responsibilities as things were getting out of hand in Khartoum. I read Hebrews with jaunts into John, Isaiah, and Psalms. I created a work schedule, but never followed it. But I had a better feel for my priorities.

I went to Treetops on Friday to watch the animals through the night. That's where Princess Elizabeth was staying when she found out her father had died and she would now be Queen Elizabeth.

Love,

L

Dear Harriet,

In June, I got in touch with a Cøllø doctor. He invited me to his home for a late lunch. I wanted to meet him to have a Cøllø contact in Nairobi in case I had to leave Khartoum. I had gone into town to shop, dressed casually. When I returned to my room, my roommate had left and locked the door. No one had a spare key. The doctor came to pick me up, and I apologized for my appearance and explained what had happened. He said he understood, and off we went to his house.

We enjoyed a pleasant visit, but at 5:00 I mentioned I should get home. The sun sets at 6:00, and I didn't want to travel at night. We got into his new car and another Cøllø lady joined us. I asked where she lived. We drove to her home first so I could see it. When we arrived, they said, "Do you wish to meet the people inside?"

"Oh, yes," I replied. So, in we went. Inside, we found two women and two men. As my friend introduced me to Dr. Lam Akol, I recognized him as the leader of one faction of the SPLA. He is a Cøllø and nephew of my friend Amos in Khartoum. When I greeted him, I said, "I've heard of you."

"I've heard of you, too."

We had a good chat, and I explained our goals for the Cøllø project and SIL. It was a great public relations exercise for me. I had the best rapport with him of all the SIL Sudan members. At one point, he asked why we didn't pay salaries to the people who worked with us. I thought for a moment and replied, "You expect me, a woman, to pay for you, a man?"

Cøllø society is very patriarchal, and they don't expect women to fund a household. That is the man's responsibility. He stared at me and replied, "You people pick your times!" I had a little smile.

Love,

L

Dear Harriet,

I left tasks for the Cølløs to do. One or two of them were to add colloquial Arabic to the Shilluk-English dictionary. Nyikwec finished teaching the primer and gave a final exam, taught another transition class, and planned the 1993 calendar. Another teacher completed the Alphabet Storybook for publication in August. Several others worked on the final edits of the Writers' Workshop Storybook. They got books on the Cøllø kings, a book of proverbs, and one of riddles ready for the committee. Hopefully, by giving them specific jobs to complete, they will take on more responsibility. After all, it is their language.

Upon my return to Khartoum, I met with a committee of Anyua people to discuss a Romanized alphabet. Anyua is a cross-border language with people living in Sudan and Ethiopia. Most languages in Ethiopia had to use the Ethiopian script, Ge'ez. But there aren't enough vowels and vowel lengths in that script. Since Anyua is closely related to Cøllø, I explained what symbols the Cølløs were using, and, as a good consultant does, offered them several alternatives. They departed to discuss the options with the other speakers in Ethiopia.

The authorities lifted the currency restrictions. Political injustice continued with churches closed, pastors arrested and detained without charge, and homes knocked down. I was told they destroyed homes to make way for a Palestinian state. *Would the Palestinians want to live here?* The war continued with no end in sight. Prices continued to increase by gigantic leaps while the exchange rate inched along. The majority suffer and no one dares to say a word.

I exchanged $700 into local currency to pay for three bicycles for the project. They gave me $400 of that in small notes worth $.10 each. It took a basket to carry it home. I stored part of it in the closet as there wasn't room anywhere else. I think the government was having a cash flow problem. At least it was paper money. If it had been coins, I'd have needed help to carry it. I asked the teachers to count out the payroll, as it's too fiddly for me and the bills are filthy.

Love,

L

Dear Harriet,

Janice returned from England. After settling in, she and three others headed to a literacy celebration. Several influential women had completed the transition course in April and now were receiving their certificates. On the way, they got caught in a huge traffic jam (two hours) because several power poles had fallen across the road and a building had collapsed after it rained. Others coming to the occasion were in the same jam, but once everyone arrived, the celebration proceeded.

Roda, our typist, traveled to Malakal and fell ill. She required an operation, but when she recovered, her mother returned to Khartoum with her. Roda reported that the schools in Malakal housed many displaced Nuer and Dinka women and children. They had no clothes, food, or medicines because the Muslims refused to give aid to non-Muslims. They were starving because they were Christians.

August 2, 1992, US News and World Report pointed out the State Department was concerned by what they saw as Iran's virtual takeover of Sudan and its stepped-up persecution of the country's three million Christians. Iran's plan was to force Christians from the south to move to the Islamic north. There they would have to send their children to Muslim schools as the government was not to allow Christian schools to open. Iran encouraged Sudan to block relief aid so that only those willing to convert to Islam received anything. Finally, they reported that much of Iran's $23 million in aid to Sudan funded terrorist training camps.

In Khartoum, the government instigated a curfew at 6:00 p.m. If you were on the street after that hour, soldiers might shoot you. Also, the power and water supplies became more problematic. One American family with seven children had electricity only two days out of six. Another couple had eight hours of power in six days. We were grateful that we lived in Mogran with regular (nearly constant) electricity and water. It makes such a difference in how much energy we have to do our work.

As my father was ill, I tried multiple times to call home. I made these international calls at the Hilton or Meridien Hotels, or at a public phone center. When I booked the call, I told them how long I wanted to talk, and at the end of that time, they cut us off. With an eight-hour time difference and my hectic schedule, connecting with them was difficult.

Love,

L

Dear Harriet,

Our brief rainy season, August, presented further challenges. It was hot, and the rain made it even more humid. Storms were short but intense.

Janice had been sick for several days. She only went from her bedroom to the bathroom and back again. She was ill so rarely that I decided to take her to the doctor, but it began to rain. The wind blew, and I knew from experience not to get out in such weather. No one would be available, including the doctor. Just then, I heard an enormous crash! Janice leapt from her bed and ran into the sitting room. It was the first sign of real life I'd seen in days. She exclaimed something fell past her window! We rushed to the kitchen door and found a 24-foot branch had broken off the nearby eucalyptus tree. It had fallen across the outside office and into the back passageway. We were thankful it did not hit the house or damage the air conditioner. I think the shock must have healed Janice, because I don't recall ever going to the doctor's office.

Later, we discovered others had experienced interesting problems as well during this time. The Luwo and Dinka translation teams wanted to produce booklets of the prophetic book of Amos from the Old Testament. First, the electricity was cut off. Then lightning struck near the office and damaged two generators, a computer, the laser printer, a fuse box, and the electricity meter. One team had left their manuscript in their office, but when they tried to retrieve it, the door refused to unlock. They explained the door had "locked itself." When they tried to reprint their work, the printer used the wrong fonts. In the end, I'm pleased to say that with determination and perseverance, both groups completed their books. What an effort!

Love,

L

Dear Harriet,

Travel to or from Sudan was never a sure thing. I remember after a visit to Nairobi, John, Pam and I checked into Kenya Airways for the flight to Khartoum. We got in just ahead of a Bermudan tour group of thirty-five headed to Egypt! We completed the formalities and were the first to arrive at the gate area. Pam and I decided, after drinking a cup of tea, to use the ladies' room and then buy a bar of chocolate. When we returned, the officials had separated the Khartoum passengers from the others. The Kenyan staff announced the plane was one and a half tons overweight. The proposed solution to this problem was (1) for 18 passengers to go on a later flight, or (2) everyone go without their luggage. No one volunteered. The third alternative was to remove the twenty-five passengers scheduled to stop in Khartoum. The Khartoum passengers were not thrilled, but they erupted when one first-class Khartoum passenger slipped out the door to the plane. The airplane landed in Khartoum to let off this one man. But I did NOT want to get on a plane that was one and a half tons overweight. I couldn't see how taking off eighteen people's luggage was going to solve that problem, at forty-four pounds per bag. So, we remained behind and Kenya Airways put us up in the Safari Club Hotel.

One of the stranded passengers was to meet former President Jimmy Carter in Khartoum and then fly on to Juba with him. This was the third time Kenya Air had canceled her flight to Khartoum. I'm not sure what happened to the Sudanese passengers. They were not in the hotel, and I fear they spent three days at the airport. That's a terrible fate.

We arrived at the hotel at 2:00 a.m. Each room was a suite with a sitting room, bedroom, and a posh bathroom. The airline paid for our meals, so John, Pam, and I vacationed in luxury.

When we returned to the airport after three days, we checked in again. John mentioned we had been terribly inconvenienced by the delay and asked if we could have an upgrade. They agreed and for the only time in my life, I flew first class. Those people travel well! I suggested next time we volunteer to stay behind and try for the upgrade!

Love,

L

Dear Harriet,

Leaving Sudan was never predictable. As a short-term visitor, departing isn't difficult, but if you have a residence permit, then the challenges begin. First, you must have an exit visa to leave. To get an exit visa, you must show you have paid your taxes and there are no warrants out for your arrest. If you plan to return, you need a reentry visa. Usually, these are obtained at the same time. A final exit visa requires more checking, so people might get the exit/reentry and not use the reentry. Our office staff took care of this process, but it was a relief when I had the correct documents stamped in my passport.

I heard of a reporter who had said uncomplimentary things about the government and faced deportation. The authorities insisted he leave the country within twenty-four hours. He arrived at the airport with a police escort to make sure he departed. At immigration, however, the officer examined his passport and noted there was no exit visa. The man could not leave the country without an exit visa, police escort or no. So, he returned home. I understand he stayed on and received a residence visa for a year. One never knew what would happen at the airport.

My friend Cathy planned to leave on a 10:30 p.m. flight to Kenya. The plane didn't arrive, so she spent the night and part of the next day at the Meridien Hotel. I visited, and we had a nice relaxing time enjoying the air conditioning.

Janice needed to fly to England at 4:15 a.m. This occurred after her sickness, dealing with the fallen tree limb, finishing the teacher's guide, and clearing up her stuff. At the airport, the agent said she had not re-confirmed her flight and wasn't on the passenger list. She nearly lost it. I think she cried. They let her check in at 3:35.

Janice recognized the daughter of a friend of ours at the check-in counter. They chatted and Mary noticed that Janice's suitcase was over the weight limit. A dozen grapefruits are heavy.

Mary said, "Oh, this suitcase is very heavy. You have to pay for the overweight!"

"How much is that?"

Mary checked the cost. Janice looked shell-shocked and said, "Oh, that is a lot of money!"

Mary thought and then asked, "Do you want to pay for it?"

Janice looked surprised and said, "No, I don't."

Before Janice could take any further action, Mary said, "Oh, all right then." She checked the bag through and it went on to England at no charge.

That incident reminded me of the time Russ took me to the airport in Kenya with a heavy foot locker. It weighed at least sixty pounds when the limit was forty-four. Russ hoisted it onto the scales and the weight read forty-four pounds. We knew it weighed more than that. The check-in person said, "Oh, it weighs over the limit because the scale is broken!"

Russ replied, "Who should I believe, you or the scale?" The man couldn't argue with that, so I didn't get charged for the overweight.

Love,

L

Dear Harriet,

In July, I learned that the Cøllø king had died. He had a goiter and was on his way to have surgery in Kuwait when Iraq invaded that country. He also had diabetes. Cøllø kings may not have any physical defects, so I guess he decided his time was at an end. He took his entourage to his home village, Pacoda, and that is where he died. According to Cøllø tradition, "The king can never die alone." What that statement means is someone has to kill him. Seven older women have this responsibility. They are called the Nyimän, the Cøllø name for the Pleiades constellation. They are to sneak into his house and strangle him. Of course, the other relatives try to prevent this from happening, but they manage to get in and do the deed. A new king has been selected but won't officially take over until April 1993.

I had a week of meetings with clergy in mid-August 1992. The Catholic bishop from Malakal had come to Khartoum on his way to Zambia for a conference. He and the archbishop had difficulty getting exit visas. Since they were delayed, I spoke with the bishop regarding a Dutch priest who was translating the Bible and creating a dictionary using the old spelling system. The bishop was not aware of this work, but he understood the problem of having new materials published in the old spelling. This could cause unnecessary division.

The priest in question had talked with me. He said, "The Shilluks have to decide how they want to spell their language."

I agreed but explained they had decided. Several Cølløs had explained the new system, but he found it "too boring" to put dots on the vowels. It may bore him, but it is essential for the Cølløs! In my opinion, he was not living out what he said he believed.

The bishop assured me nothing would be published without his approval, and the implication was that he wouldn't approve it unless it was in the new spelling.

Love,

L

Dear Harriet,

I made up a new song: "We love living in Khartoum (2x). Each and every day is new in some new way. We love living in Khartoum."

Anne and Craig invited us to have coffee at the Hilton Hotel, as they had matters to discuss and wanted to talk in comfort. So, we agreed to meet them and sit in the air conditioning. On the way over, as Janice and I bounced along the half-mile to the Hilton, I noticed the sky looked strange. I pointed out the dust hanging on the underside of the clouds and Janice said, "If this were England, I would say it is going to snow!"

"I don't think so!" I replied and felt sweat running down my back. It was 110°F and humid.

We parked the car and entered the blissful cool of the air-conditioned hotel. Anne and Craig met us and we took a tour of the shops before having our coffee. We enjoyed the little bakery shop at the far end of the lobby near the double doors. These doors served as the VIP entrance and were not open to the public. A twenty-foot overhang allowed cars to drive up and deliver their important passengers. No VIPs came in that day, so we examined the elaborately frosted cakes and pastries for sale. They always look better than they taste.

Just as we got our coffee, the wind began to blow. We tried to have a serious conversation, but it was difficult. Outside the fifteen-foot windows, the palm trees bent at right angles and plastic bags whizzed past like bullets. Soon the dust arrived, and the world turned a sandy shade of yellow and brown. The rain that followed was not a little sprinkle, but a deluge the likes of which I have rarely seen. The wind blew sideways with such force that the power went out. An emergency generator started, and within minutes, it blew up. A second emergency generator struggled to stay on, lights blinking on and off. A crowd gathered at the far end of the lobby near the shop, so we investigated. The hotel staff had grabbed huge towels to mop up the tidal wave flowing in through the closed double doors. The rain blew straight at them despite the overhang, flooding the floor in an inch of water. We watched in amazement.

Anne frantically called home because her ten-year-old son was there alone. Charlie was in the front yard with their tortoise. The front yard was lower than the porch and filled with water. The tortoise was so heavy, Charlie couldn't lift him out of the water, so he just held its head up so it wouldn't drown. We decided to get home as quickly as possible.

Getting home was more of a challenge than we had expected. First, we had to wade through the parking lot to the car. In that short time, the streets flooded with at least six inches of water. In places, it was even deeper. On our street, we could no longer see the ditch (four-feet deep). It was wall-to-wall water! Our Suzuki's high wheelbase helped, so we put her in four-wheel drive and traversed the road by memory, making lots of waves as we moved along. I parked outside the gate and waded to the house. Water was halfway up my calf.

Inside, we found three Cølløs huddled in the sitting room. They were sipping cups of tea, having moved the furniture away from the leaks in the ceiling. Water ran down the walls in a stream, so they took the clock and pictures off the walls. There was no power. On the back verandah, our washing machine sat in water, two inches deep. The Cølløs rushed home to see if their homes and families had been affected. As far as I know, everyone survived.

Anne and Craig later told me it took them two hours to traverse the city to their house. At one point, they drove INTO a drainage ditch so full of water it was not visible. The water often came to the tops of the wheels of their Suzuki. It was like driving across three to four miles of a shallow lake to get home. Their housekeeper helped Charlie lift the tortoise to safety. Few will forget that rain.

Love,

L

———————

Dear Harriet,

Would you ever have expected to pay $50 for a crate of empty Pepsi bottles? Well, that was one of the essential items in Khartoum in the early 1990s. The shops sold sodas, and we could buy one and drink it there, leaving the bottle. However, if we wanted to take the drink home, we had to give them an empty bottle. Hospitality protocol involved offering a cold soft drink to a visitor. It became mandatory to have at least half a case of sodas on hand. So, when we discovered a crate of empty Pepsi or Fanta bottles for sale, we snapped them up. In the end, we had three crates of drink bottles as we couldn't exchange a Pepsi bottle for a Fanta. Sometimes we had so many visitors that we ran through a crate of drinks in a single week. Remember, we rarely drank a soft drink. These were just for company.

In August 1992, the Cøllø Language Oversight Committee told us the Cøllø language area now had its own province, called Pacoda. The headquarters were in Wada Kona, which is 20 km southwest of Renk. Since people only spoke Cøllø and some limited Arabic there, the committee thought the commissioner of the province needed to know about the literacy project. To gain his support, they arranged a meeting at our house. The committee turned up on time and the commissioner came forty-five minutes later for our hour-and-a-half meeting. After hearing about our work, he offered to contribute £s10,000 ($1,000 in those days) to the project, along with a plot of land in Wada Kona for a center. Also, he agreed to provide local materials for building it and thought we should purchase a motorcycle. He told one of his people to take the bicycles and blackboards we had purchased to Wada Kona and Renk. It was a successful meeting and well worth the case of sodas, four pounds of bananas, three packages of cookies, and one and a half pounds of sugar. I don't know how much tea we used. Acol and Roda (the typist) oversaw the kitchen chores during the meeting so we could concentrate on the discussion.

Love,

L

Dear Harriet,

As I continued working, I was waiting to hear from my parents. Weeks passed with no letter. I tried phoning but never caught them at home.

Mr. J from the J-language came to work with me once a week. I made the least progress with him. Three other groups met me every two weeks and worked independently. A language committee has formed with the A-Team, so that is progress. The Cølløs kept me busy the rest of the time.

Janice has four Cølløs helping her revise the primer, and they are doing a great job. She revises the lessons and prints them out. Each version improves the quality! The Alphabet Storybook, in process for one and a half years, should be ready for a final check in a month. The teachers created an easy-to-read book describing cultural events during the Cøllø year. It uses the pictures from this year's calendar with expanded text. We have the 1993 calendar ready along with a new hymnbook, a book of Proverbs, and stories from workshops. For a few hours, I work on the dictionary. On our "day off" we teach the grammar workshop.

On Sundays, I take part in the worship team at the International Church. That provides some light relief as it revives my spirit and puts me back on an even keel.

Love,

L

Dear Harriet,

The electricity became erratic on our line. I went to the nearby electricity company to complain. After several days of this, I took Peter M, as his Arabic is better than mine. As he headed inside, four Mercedes arrived. Arab men exited the cars and entered the customer service door. They came to complain about the same issue. They said, "We are tired of this on and off power. Don't just turn it on now, FIX the problem so this doesn't keep happening!"

After that, when the power cut off, I stuck my head out the door and asked Peter M, "Do you think the Mercedes will take care of this?"

He answered, "Yes."

We sat tight and soon the power returned.

Love,

L

Dear Harriet,

We began the grammar course in late August for Nilotic languages: Dinka, Nuer, Cøllø, Mabaan, and Luwo. Each of these groups had Bible translation work in progress. So, this workshop was to discover the grammatical structure of these languages. We met each Friday for three months. Most businesses close on Friday, so we worked during the morning and into the afternoon. The speakers know their grammar subconsciously, but we hope to bring the structures to a conscious level and give them the vocabulary to describe it. After the first month, we were on the brink of figuring out something that has plagued linguistics for decades: the word order!

I became the Linguistic Coordinator for Khartoum. As I was working with five languages, we needed a plan to meet the demand other than "Leoma will do it." When I asked for help, the administration said, "You are just ahead of the planning," and I said, "The planning is too slow for the demand."

John and Pam moved to Khartoum after he finished his PhD. I wrote a seven-page report on what I was doing and explained the people's expectations. I have involved other teams in my work, but we need to figure out a long-term solution.

In case we needed more stress, our visa sponsor lost their status, so the administration is hunting for another official organization to sponsor us.

One of the pastor/translators was arrested (no charge brought against him). They held him incommunicado for two weeks.

Janice and I attended a Cøllø Cultural Day and had a delightful time. I think Sudan television filmed us during the evening performance. We sat in the second row behind the dignitaries.

I got a letter from my parents. My father had surgery and was in the hospital for a week. I need to move up my plans to go home.

Love,

L

Dear Harriet,

After seeing a specialist, my parents phoned me on October 2. I learned that my father had only a short time to live, and if I wanted to see him, I needed to get home. I booked a flight, got my exit/reentry visa and was home a week later. All thoughts of workshops and language groups flew out of my head. My family was my priority.

Once I was home, we followed the doctor's advice and made a short trip to The Apple Barn. We bought some delicious fried apple pies and as we munched on them, we tried to converse. Dad was not in the mood to talk. Before, he would have been the life of the party. When we got home, he was tired. He went upstairs to rest and never walked out of the bedroom again.

We called for hospice as Dad often had spells on the weekend! Hospice was such a blessing. They provided everything we needed and were on call at any time. On November 9, my father passed away. My parents had been married fifty-one years and were best friends.

Mom and I were in shock for weeks after the funeral. We depended on each other for comfort and support. I was grateful for the many who prayed for me during that time. I received several notes and messages from Sudanese friends offering their condolences.

Love,

L

Dear Harriet,

Here is a letter I wrote to my father before he died:

Dearest Dad,

Over the last ten years, it seems we've both gotten better at saying things on paper than in words. So, I thought I might be able to express some of my deep love for you more easily on paper, and besides, it stays around to be re-read.

Remember how you used to take me swimming for hours and hours? You taught me how to swim: flippers first with an inner tube, then no inner tube, then one flipper, and finally setting me free with only my own skills. It's always been my best sport and I still enjoy it regularly. I can still see us in the canoe that afternoon when I jumped out to swim to shore, and you were trying to see how tight a turn you could make in the canoe. It threw you out and went sailing across the lake. You had on your heavy work shoes, jeans, and pockets full of coins and keys. It didn't occur to me at the time you might have drowned. But you made it to shore, and I recovered the canoe.

Remember the Florida vacations, the hurricane, Harriet's many boyfriends, crabbing (especially the one that got your toe!), learning to dive in the pool, my terrifying drive in the cars at Jekyll Island, the VW trip where we packed in beach towels and brought back those chalk portraits through that deluge. We proved the car was waterproof.

Remember picking me up at school and taking me to the train station? You set up the mailbags and stuck in labels while I played with anything that moved. I felt so special to have that time with you.

I remember trying to walk down the tracks and not being good at it. I still wonder how train wheels stay on. During all my years, I've never felt that your work was more important than I was. I guess inside I knew I was Number One with you.

You courageously taught me how to drive and I've done a lot of safe driving—a few stupid things too, but on the whole, I haven't been a danger. I never did so well with the boat.

Then there are the flapdoodles. During my stay in Africa, I've been amazed at how flashes of ideas have come to me, giving me ideas of how to fix things, and the image has been when I was watching you. I didn't think I'd watched that intently or with that much comprehension, but it seems I did. I almost always make some effort to repair the problem before I call in our repairmen. At least with that experience, I can give them a more pinpoint description of the exact nature of the problem. I'm the one who keeps our car checked for oil, water, etc. I see a lot of you in me.

You are a great storyteller and I've learned the art from you. You even have a following in Sudan. I read your letters to people and they always enjoyed them. Often, I'm asked if you've written. They want to hear another tale or two. Many have expressed a desire to meet you, sure they would get along well from the first.

I learned to get to the point and not wander about in useless words. Be precise and concise. I'm known for my humor, and that, too, was one of your many contributions. I learned what made you laugh, and the world laughs too.

And like you, I learned to use my storytelling as a protection. As the teller-of-tales, you control the flow of the conversation, so no one feels uncomfortable—least of all you (or me). If people are having a good time, they won't be tempted to bring up unpleasant topics or ask embarrassing questions. Are you surprised? Don't be. Who could know you better than one who is so like you? It's a gentle confinement that most people don't notice, and for those of us who are shy and fearful, it is a safe haven, and people think we are outgoing.

I share many of your good points: gentleness, patience, compassion, humor, even your intelligence and good looks! I'm proud to be your daughter and grateful for the chance to tell you so. Janice's father died before she could say goodbye. I'm glad—forever thankful—that I can say on paper, in words, and in actions: I love you! And I'm proud to be your little girl.

With much more love than you will ever know.

Love,

L

Dear Harriet,

Work didn't stop because I wasn't there. Janice carried on bravely. She kept me posted on the latest news by mail.

At the end of the grammar workshop, each group made presentations of their findings. I wish I could have heard those. Otto took the lead for the Cølløs in my absence and kept them on the right track.

On the work front, Janice took Roda and Peter M to the office to help produce more books. Three teachers have registered 80+ students, and we didn't have enough books for that many students. Otto has 45 students, none of whom could read at all. They start with the Alphabet Book, then the pre-primer (sight word storybook). Once they have completed those, they are ready for the primer. She sent the 1993 calendars to the printer. The office purchased a risograph! Oh, what a difference that made! No more stencils and spirit-led Gestetner to deal with! The risograph works like a fancy photocopier, but a lot faster.

A risograph machine

A new member, Ruth, stayed with Janice for several weeks while looking for a house in Mogran. Once she found one, it needed repairs. Her presence provided significant support because working so hard and keeping a house running and food on the table is not a straightforward task. For example, the car battery died. Janice asked our maintenance guys to investigate the problem. They found two things wrong: a regulator and the earth cable had broken. They thought the battery might be okay. The cable and regulator were replaced, and the car ran fine that day, but the battery was dead the next morning. She purchased a new battery only to discover the posts were too big for our connectors. The guys modified the leads to fit, but she wished she had simply had the battery fitted when it first died.

Janice purchased a much-needed four-drawer file cabinet and a desk chair. She was in a workshop or in staff meetings or getting books and calendars printed up to the time she left Khartoum to be with her mother over Christmas.

Before leaving for England, Janice and Peter M ran a production workshop. It is one thing to write stories and edit them, but when you have to turn them into a book, that's a distinct set of knowledge. They went over how to determine the size, put in the pictures, space, and size the written words. Then they learned to make a mock-up so you know which pages should align.

Politically, the church leaders were experiencing challenges. The authorities released the pastor/translator they had detained for two months without a trial. He said they treated him well. He planned to marry before Christmas. Another of the Presbyterian pastors, Ezekiel, boarded a flight to Cyprus. Security took him off the plane and when they brought his suitcase, it was empty. Someone had stolen his clothes. When the Catholic bishop returned from Rome, the security services met him and escorted him home. Rumors suggested the Pope might visit Sudan in the New Year. So, the government wanted to "keep in" with the Catholics.

Amid the pressure and busyness in this very hot place, it would be easy to give up and go home for a more comfortable life. But an unseen force keeps you there despite the difficulties. I came to appreciate Don McClure's words:

> "I love the Sudan. It is easy to see why so many missionaries call this their real home. Here life, and each day, demands everything you have. I was discouraged at first because the need is so great that meeting it seems hopeless. Missionaries here are not overworked by heavy duties, but are overwhelmed by innumerable trifles. I am usually disgusted with what I haven't been able to accomplish, but it is a joy to give my all. Everything we do is really appreciated."

> "Today it is 112 degrees in the shade, and the wind off the desert is like the breath of a furnace. The other day a sandstorm, or haboob, struck us. It would be hard to imagine the magnificence of the tremendous cloud that enshrouded everything. It looked as if a genie had opened a magic jar and released red and amber smoke. We saw a solid wall of

sand about three hundred feet high and ten miles wide. The first part soared over our heads, and then we were struck by all its fury. We could feel the house quiver as sand blasted against it. The air was so fiery hot that doors had to be left open. Our hair was stiff, breathing was difficult, and ears and mouths were filled. Now I know what it means to get a taste of the country." (Partee, 27.)

Love,

L

————

Dear Harriet,

Our typist, Roda, fell on hard times because of family problems. She had worked with us for three years without returning home to Malakal. With several children needing food, clothing, and school fees, she "took permission" to travel home for a month. She told us an amazing story upon her return.

Roda had worked as a typist in a government office in the state capital, Malakal, before moving to Khartoum. She had "taken permission" from them to visit Khartoum. That visit lasted several years. When she returned, she greeted her relatives and acquaintances, and then turned up to her old office. She sat at her desk and explained that she was back at work and annoyed they had stopped paying her during her absence. She was present now, so they should compensate her for the missed salary and for the current work.

Roda at the computer

The administration agreed for reasons beyond my understanding. They paid her back wages and put her to work. Once she settled her claim, she worked for three weeks. She then "took permission" from her job and returned to Khartoum. Her old job continued to pay her, although she had only turned up for work for three weeks in the past three years.

Why should she expect payment when she wasn't doing any work? Why did her employer agree to pay it? As she told me this story, she had no qualms about doing this. It was her due, and she had claimed what was rightfully hers, at least in her eyes. I suspect she is not the only person who used this ploy to their own advantage.

If the Sudanese government is going broke, this practice may explain why.

Love,

L

Chapter 6:
1993

Dear Harriet,

Mom and I made it through the holidays, but it would be a year of coming and going. In mid-January, I returned to Khartoum to renew my residence visa. If you are out of the country when those expire, it's hard to get a new one. Our situation was precarious at best, so I didn't want to risk losing it. Mom started a computer class at the local community college to give her something else to focus on. It was not the right time as she developed a phobia about computers, even Macs.

I jumped into work with both feet. I had back-to-back meetings, a workshop in progress, and catching up with the various language teams. They each produced a list of things they needed me to do. Roda had family problems and felt ill, so she was unable to do as much as we had hoped. One of the committee members gave a talk on funding at the writer's workshop. He explained Sudan had 200 percent inflation, but in a funding proposal, you must assume only 25 percent for inflation and do the best you can with what you get. The Cøllø team had made good progress. We were encouraged that they were taking on more responsibility.

The A-Team disagreed about the alphabet. The community, and therefore the committee, have two dialects. There is a main street in the village and those who live on one side speak a certain way, and the others speak a slightly different way. They have fought over that for years without a resolution.

Janice returned and settled in. We visited our Sudanese friends and passed out the goodies we had brought back. Many gave us a meal even though prices are higher than ever. The temperature is comfortable at 60°-80°F. As the Linguistic Coordinator, I met with the other coordinators to work out the workshop schedule for the next eighteen months.

Love,

L

Dear Harriet,

February 10 found me sitting on the curb of a sidewalk in the Green Square. The Green Square was built for Islamic rallies, but this time, I, along with a million others, was there to see Pope John Paul II. We learned the churches had requested buses to bring people from the outlying areas to welcome the Pope, but the government refused. People came anyway and lined the streets waving palm leaves as the Pope rode into town from the airport. The Muslims saw this display and asked, "Is this how it will be at the end of time?"

I had a red guest badge with his picture on it. Our tickets promised chairs, but since we only arrived forty minutes early, our seats were taken, so I was sitting on a curb. The surrounding people provided a bit of shade, as there wasn't a tree in sight. Everyone had to be in place an hour before he arrived, and no one could leave until fifteen minutes after he departed. We expected the program to last until 7:00 p.m. The temperature has been in the 60s at night, so I brought a sweater, jacket, scarf, hose, and socks. People were quiet and well organized. Security was high, as they feared a terrorist attack by fundamentalists. Jo had invited us for lunch before the event and made placemats with "Welcome Pope John Paul II" written on them!

The power went out in the middle of the program, and the Pope was the whitest thing visible. We held our breath, but nothing happened and the power was soon restored. It was a powerful experience to see that many Christians in one place in Khartoum. Most southerners are Christian rather than Muslim. There were so many displaced people living on the outskirts of the capital that Christians outnumbered Muslims in the Khartoum census. During the mass, a Sudanese lady showed me a picture of the Pope and said, "Who is this?" Clearly, not everyone knew why they were there.

We left early to avoid the rush. As we departed, we saw children playing and singing, women making tea, and six Muslims praying while the mass was in progress. What a contrast.

Love,

L

Dear Harriet,

Janice put together the Writer's Course Storybook with Peter M using the new risograph and finishing in under three hours. The workshop only had six participants, but four Cølløs were on staff. Our strategy was for people to attend the course first. The next time we offered it, they helped teach. Once they gained confidence and experience, they ran the course.

During this time, I planned the next workshop to teach phonology for September and October. I outlined all the lectures, twenty-one in total. This workshop is for our Nilotic teams: Cøllø, Dinka, Nuer,

Luwo, and Mabaan. Some of them have not finalized their writing systems, so we thought the in-depth training might help them resolve the remaining issues.

My residence visa and exit/reentry visas came through. As a bonus, Janice and I signed the papers to get the title of the car transferred to our names. After four years, it was time. That total process cost $350.

As I prepared to return home, each Sudanese I spoke to affirmed the importance of spending time with my mother. As I am an only child, it was essential. It is inconceivable to them that anyone would choose to live alone. In a Sudanese home, a young child would come and stay with an older adult to do the household chores and provide company. I could see they were struggling to understand our strange ways.

Love,

L

Dear Harriet,

I arrived in Chattanooga on February 22 with a plan to spend time with my family and to visit my supporters and supporting churches. At the beginning of March, a Knoxville church held their annual conference. I attended the first half. The weather was warm and spring-like. However, I was expected at another conference in Montgomery, Alabama, the second half of that week. So, I flew there to attend. The person who picked me up from the airport mentioned that a severe storm was coming through and I arrived just in time. The first night of the conference went well, but then the storm hit. We had thunder-snow. I had never heard thunder with snow, but that night I experienced it. Montgomery received 3" of snow for the first time since 1901. We continued the conference through the weekend, but with lower attendance than normal. Then it was time to fly home, but the airports were closed. After two days, I flew to Atlanta and stayed with a friend. Chattanooga got 21" of snow—unheard of in my lifetime. The mountains had three feet!

Mom's electricity went off and the fire insert Dad installed worked on electricity. A neighbor helped get her to a house with power. She stayed there while I tried to get home. Once the airport opened, I flew in, but there wasn't room to stay where Mom was. So, the same neighbor arranged for us to make use of an apartment that was unoccupied. I think the couple who lived there was getting a divorce. They had left, but not yet taken the furniture. Mom and I stayed there for several days. Once we could get to the house and the power was restored, we settled back at home. That was an adventure and not one I care to repeat.

On one of my trips to a conference in Georgia, I stayed with Phyllis. She and I just hit it off. After the meetings finished, I had a couple of days, and she let me spend them at her house. We binge-watched TV shows and videos. At the end of that time, she presented me with the Couch Potato Award in recognition of my remarkable ability to do nothing for incredible periods of time.

Love,

L

Dear Harriet,

Meanwhile, Janice and Chris were having their own adventure, a trip to Karima. This was Janice's first trip outside of Khartoum. They took a four-day journey with the Sudan Archeological Society.

Twenty-nine people of various nationalities traveled on a "bus." It was a converted Bedford truck with lots of projecting pieces of metal to lacerate the unwary. Janice had wanted to travel on one but doesn't wish to do it again.

They left the house at 5:30 a.m. By the time the crew loaded and strapped down the luggage, food, and water, it was 7:00. In the first three hours, they got stuck once in the sand and had three flat tires, always the same wheel. With only one spare, repairs took place on the spot. The crew attached an air pump to the battery to reinflate the tire.

There was more vegetation in the desert than she expected. Hills covered in black rocks looked like tip heaps in a coalfield. There were camels, goats, and a good number of people living in tents made of goat hair.

They stopped at a tea stop and paid inflated prices. Fortunately, Janice and Chris had taken sandwiches, oranges, and drinking water. There were no conveniences, so one had to find a bush for one's private business.

After getting stuck in the sand twenty times, they didn't make it to Karima that day. At 6:15, the sun was setting. They stopped and camped in the desert. Janice had a thin foam mattress, a sleeping bag, and a blanket to protect her from the cold, nasty wind. The water in their thermos was still hot, so a tomato Cup-a-Soup tasted good. The crew put kerosene lanterns out so passengers wouldn't get run over as there was no official road. The stars were fabulous. In the morning, two people found scorpions in their shoes.

Along the way, they saw the remains of a large Christian monastery and a few small pyramids at Nuri. At 5:30 p.m., they crossed the Nile by ferry to reach Karima. They planned to stay at a technical school, but none of the staff knew of any arrangement. So, they ended up at the canning factory rest house. That factory makes tomato paste when tomatoes are in season.

The rooms were stuffy, so Chris and Janice slept on comfortable beds in the garden.

The next day, they visited Jebel Barkal. This was a temple complex associated with Taharqa, one of the five Sudanese pharaohs. Bits of the original painting were visible. There were also a few small pyramids.

The following morning, they were up at 3:00 a.m. and on their way by 4:00. The passengers received a free shower as water containers on the roof leaked inside as the bus bounced along. They reached Khartoum at 6:00 p.m. It looked like a large, green, sophisticated city! They arrived home at 7:00 and luxuriated in a warm shower and a comfortable bed.

Love,

L

Dear Harriet,

May 10 came too soon for my mother, as I returned to Khartoum. Reentry visas are only valid for three months. I wasn't looking forward to arriving in May after a pleasant spring.

On my way back, I stopped in Amsterdam to see the Keukenhof. It is the largest flower garden in the world, and is only open fifty days a year, from Easter to Pentecost. What an amazing place. God's creativity shows in the colors, shapes, and sizes of these gorgeous flowers. The Dutch know how to show them to their best advantage. I bought two posters to put up in Khartoum to remind me there is such beauty.

I arrived at Khartoum airport with my two heavy suitcases. The woman customs officer checked through my things and found my dry cat food. She asked what it was. I explained I owned two cats and brought the food for them. She asked, "Oh, do you live here?"

"Yes," I replied. She smiled, closed my suitcases, stuck the customs stickers on them and sent me on my way.

Janice met me at the airport and took me straight to the office, as she had work to do. The fuel ration was up to three gallons this week. A Cøllø who works for the oil company brought us a gallon from his allowance, so we could function. The government severely rationed fuel during this time. One week, we got two gallons, but heard that later in the week, people with ration cards didn't get any. The maintenance staff had collected our allowance of fuel for us during our five weeks in Kenya, so that put us ten gallons ahead.

There was still a lot of work, even though it never cooled down below 100°F at night and often reached 120°F (50°C) in the shade during the day. I needed to discern the important from the urgent. At least the electricity was constant. When the temperature is 90°–105°F in the house, I normally drink 2 eight-ounce glasses of water in four gulps. We refilled the gallon and a half water jug several times a day, especially when visitors came. Just keeping ahead on filtered water and ice was a challenge.

I hoped Mom was staying busy. I reminded her, "Keep your courage up and look to the Shepherd. He's always there and he always cares about everything."

Love,

L

Dear Harriet,

We went to the American Club for lunch about 3:00 p.m. They had their own challenges, as it took them an hour and a half to serve our food. As soon as we had eaten, we headed home.

It was a good thing we arrived when we did. Our landlady's relatives had cleared out some things in her rooms. They piled the junk they didn't want by our gate and set it alight. Unfortunately, they burned it on top of the PVC water pipe to our neighbor Chris' house. There was one water meter for two households. A T-joint on our side of the meter allowed both houses to get water. If we turned off the water, no one would have any. Chris' hose sprayed water everywhere from the burned holes. The relatives left the water spewing into the yard. By the time we arrived, the yard was flooded, with more water running into the street. What a mess! It took two hours to get the water stopped to her house while keeping it on in ours. After a week, we got the pipe replaced, though the new joints leaked for several days!

Leoma clearing the rubbish off the burned hose

We felt oppressed by our minor problems, but our difficulties didn't compare with what my friends endured. Many southerners had settled in displacement camps around the city. But, the government decided the southerners should move further out of the city. New development plans provided an excuse for this destruction. People normally were given a few days' warning, but on the appointed day, bulldozers arrived along with the police, and the houses were flattened. If they were lucky and prepared, the people rescued their possessions. Sometimes lorries transported the people and their goods to the new desert area. At other times, the people paid for this transportation. In all cases, the authorities left them in the most desolate areas with no water, shelter, or anything. The government posted guards to make sure they didn't return to their former homes.

I remember a BBC reporter trying to describe the situation. His colleague didn't seem to "get it" and asked, "Do you mean there are no toilets in the area?" The reporter almost shouted, "No, there aren't any toilets! There isn't ANYTHING there." The report ended, and it was obvious his colleagues in London still hadn't understood the situation.

Meanwhile, the civil war continued in the south. "The government of the north, which seeks to fashion an Islamic country, is fighting non-Muslim rebels in the south. The southerners historically have been oppressed by the north, and they resent the Arab culture's rule over their traditional African ways.

"But the southern rebels also have turned on each other. When not fighting the government, they have clashed in grabs for power, for territory and to satisfy old tribal grudges.

"The fighting has whisked more than 3 million people about the countryside like wind-blown leaves. They have been forced from one temporary haven to the next." (*The Denver Post*, May 9, 1993.)

Love,

L

Dear Harriet,

In June, we hosted a teacher training course for using the new primer. Ten participants and three Cøllø instructors came to the house. A few other people turned up, so we served breakfast to nineteen people.

The temperature in the house was rarely under 100°F. If it was, it felt positively cool! Outside temperatures have been 120°-130°F in the shade. It thundered and soon began to rain—in June. All of us stood outside to watch the rain. The temperature drops; there's a pleasant breeze. No wonder rain is considered a sign of blessing.

It seems Sudan didn't pay their phone bill because no calls were going out or coming in. No mail arrived either. Rumors abounded that the government had run out of hard currency and had "borrowed" all hard currency deposits from the banks. My bank refused to comply. Instead, they handed out bank checks to their depositors. The government withdrew their license. Exciting and unexpected events around money happen often here.

It is hard to remember that just a few weeks ago, I was enjoying time with my mom. Now, I'm catching up on my work. Here's a list of responsibilities: (1) reading monthly reports from language teams in Khartoum and commenting on them. If they need linguistic help, I should provide it. (2) I'm supervising three people learning Arabic. (3) Two to three Cøllø books are nearly ready for publication. (4) Janice is making sure the testing of the primer is going well. (5) I'm helping the A-team figure out spelling rules. (6) The three-month phonology workshop begins in October and I'm the primary instructor. (7) Janice and I are planning the intermediate writer's course for the Cølløs. (8) I've learned to write project proposals to raise money for the Cøllø work and keep track of the current accounts. You know how hopeless I am with numbers! (9) One elder is writing a paper on Cøllø culture and I'm editing it. (10) Between us, we keep food in the house, eat, cook, live, and sleep! HELP!

Janice is leaving soon to spend time with her mother. She won't be back until September. I don't know how I will keep my head above water while she's away. At the end of June, our group has a spiritual retreat and a literacy seminar in Kenya. I planned a much-needed vacation.

Love,

L

Dear Harriet,

Here are comments I overheard during the hot season:

If you want to wash clothes at 100°F or cooler, you would have to put a refrigeration unit on the washing machine.

Q. Why is there such a buildup of ice in the back of the refrigerator one week after defrosting the freezer?

A. Humidity.

Q. Why are the batteries failing to charge?

A. Dust on the solar panels

Q. Why don't the evaporative air coolers work better?

A. Humidity

Q. It feels cool in here! What is the temperature?

A. 104°F

The chair is hot, the table is hot, even my clothes are hot when I put them on!

It's time to go to Kenya for a break.

Love,

L

Dear Harriet,

Roda, our typist, had seven children and was expecting the eighth. She had only one boy. Boys are highly valued in African society. So, her husband took another wife, hoping to have more sons. When Roda asked if he had another woman, he denied it. Meanwhile, the second wife was four months pregnant. To change the subject, he complained Roda misused his money. He also accused her of sleeping with another man. We had given her a watch, and he assumed her lover had given it to her. She left the house saying, "One can die suddenly there."

She returned home just as her husband moved his new wife into her house. He expected Roda to take care of her when she delivered the baby. In these situations, we feel out of our depth to know how to respond.

The other constant in my mind was how my mother was doing. She went to Europe on a tour with my aunt. At home, she taught a Sunday School class at church. I wrote to her: "I'm glad you are going out to be with others. It is good for you even though it is hard to come home to an empty house. Those are the times when I like to see Jesus as a person—to talk to and share with—even though it seems that I'm alone. He has promised to be a husband to the widow."

Love,

L

Dear Harriet,

I wore cotton and nothing but cotton. If there was any polyester or man-made fiber in my clothes, I noticed it. In the hottest time of the year, I couldn't wear silk because the humidity made it cling to me like a plastic bag. Even the mattresses and chair cushions needed to be cotton. When the top of my pillow got too hot, I turned it over because the side next to the mattress was still cool.

Humidity was our worst enemy. The Sudanese even complained about the heat when the humidity rose. In the winter, the humidity would be 10 to 20 percent, but in summer it rose to 60 percent. That's when people used to write and say, "Oh, but it's a dry heat..." "Rubbish!" I say! In the rainy season, the temperatures dropped to the low hundreds instead of 120°F in the shade, but the humidity hit 90 percent. I felt like an oily puddle. Every ounce of energy or motivation died, and I just swam through the day, hoping for winter.

One of those hot days, as I left for town, Peter M opened the gate for me. He greeted me with, "Winter is here; the wind changed!" That was the key to the seasons: wind from the north signaled winter, and from the south, summer. The temperature, at least initially, was irrelevant. A southerly wind started in March and ended in mid-November.

We noticed the temperature change the most when we left the country. I got used to the toilet seat being hot when I sat on it. So, getting on a plane and sitting down on a cold seat was quite a shocking and revealing experience. Now you know why I wore jeans, socks, and a sweater while you and the rest of the family had on shorts and T-shirts and fanned.

Love,

L

Dear Harriet,

On one journey from Nairobi, Kenya, to Khartoum, we made a stopover in Jeddah, Saudi Arabia. During the hour and a half we were there, the cleaners came on board to spruce up the plane. All the continuing passengers had been told to stay in their seats, so that's where I was. I was not wearing a scarf on my head, but had dressed modestly for my arrival in Khartoum. However, I became increasingly uncomfortable as I thought the male cleaners were mentally undressing me. Apparently, my clothing wasn't modest enough for Saudi Arabia.

The other thing I noted during our brief layover was the shape of the luggage. Suitcases are rectangular, but not those leaving Jeddah. I've now invented the term "The Saudi Suitcase." Instead of being flat, the sides bulge until they are round. They could roll them aboard the plane. How the cases stayed closed for the journey, I do not know. Many of those people got stopped at customs in Khartoum and were asked to spread their goods out on the floor for inspection. People brought stock for their shops, so they likely got charged duty.

The other significant luggage was the carry-on passengers brought with them. Whatever happened to "one piece that fits in the overhead bin"? The person in the seat next to me wanted to put her large water container under my feet. I said, "No, thanks!" Their multiple bags blocked the aisles, filling every available space. It required an extra half hour before the Kenya Airways staff cleared the aisle. With a sigh of relief, we got airborne before the end of the runway. It may be a shopping paradise, but I have no desire to go there!

Love,

L

Dear Harriet,

We had an earthquake at 2:00 a.m. That was surprising and frightening! I leapt out of bed and stood in the doorway, trying to remember if that was the right thing to do. Then I began to question myself. *Had I imagined it?* I walked outside to see if Peter M had noticed it. Yes, it happened. By then it was over, so I returned to bed.

I'm experiencing depression, grieving for Dad. I'm also anxious about the work I need to do next week. Each day, I discuss with God what I should do, and that's what I concentrate on. When I get God's list finished, the day is over.

Nyikwec sent a letter from the south, as he is at the coronation for the new *rädh* (king). There are a huge number of people wanting books and classes, and it adds to my feelings of inadequacy. Peter M helps me with so many things, but he is heading to Renk to teach teacher training workshops and see his family. I'll miss him.

I'm using my Mac more and finding the special characters much easier to access. Cathy and I are writing a linguistic paper on topic, focus, and word order in Shilluk. All the examples must be written in phonetics.

I'm teaching Peter M to use the PC, and while it is time-consuming, he is learning. The hardest part for a Sudanese is telling a machine to do something, and it responds, sometimes saying "no."

One of my language groups asked why I was in Khartoum suffering with them and they hadn't paid me anything. I explained about God's calling and they understood that. Then they wanted to know why I hadn't brought my mom back with me. I explained the medical care here wasn't so good. They understood that too! I thought it was lovely that they felt concern for me and my mother, especially when they have so many troubles of their own.

Love,

L

———————

Dear Harriet,

August 1993—I looked around my desk at all the tasks waiting for me. Here's a list in no particular order:

- Type up a test for the primer
- Type a book of one hundred pages in English on Cøllø marriage customs
- Format the Alphabet Storybook for final printing
- Photocopy the pictures for the storybook and sizing them for printing
- Write lectures for a phonology course I start teaching in early Sept. I've done six of twenty-five so far
- Make handouts for the students
- Plan the things we need for the course like food, money, paper, folders, pencils, chalk
- Communicate with those who are to teach with me
- Write letters of invitation to those who should attend
- Keep in touch with my mother and with Janice
- Take in film for processing—pictures taken by our language officer of the coronation of the new Cøllø king

- Make another one hundred copies of the first twenty-four lessons of the primer because the ones we had have been distributed, and more are needed

- Help plan for the 1994 calendar for the Cølløs

- Work on a language that is having problems with their spelling because of different dialects

- Set the agenda for the literacy project committee meeting and for staff meetings with the teachers

- Read through the draft of a book on Cøllø songs and poetry which was completed by four men during a recent workshop

- I've also become the acting Linguistic Coordinator for the Sudan teams across four countries, while the real one is away for several months

Besides those activities, I have to run the household: shopping, cooking, etc. Many people come to talk, and it is important to listen and pray with them. Sometimes I venture to offer advice. People are struggling with living just now.

Love,

L

Dear Harriet,

Isn't communication a wonderful thing, at least when it works? I've had interesting experiences helping the Cøllø guys get their books and calendars done. In 1993, they wanted to prepare a calendar for 1994 and they needed them ready by Christmas day. People always sell calendars at church on Christmas.

Anyway, they wanted to have twelve months with thirty days in each month. This system follows the lunar months of twenty-eight days. I asked them if their year moved ahead each year, as the Islamic calendar does. They assured me it didn't but stayed the same.

The Ethiopian calendar has 12 thirty-day months and a thirteenth one that is very short. In that way, they follow lunar months, but the thirteenth month keeps them from losing days of the year. The Cølløs assured me there was no thirteenth month. So, I asked what they did with the other five days, since 30 times 12 equals 360 and there are 365 days in a year. They looked at me blankly and assured me, there were no extra five days. In the end, they compromised, and we created a western calendar with the varying number of days in a month.

On another occasion, we were trying to put pictures in a storybook. The story told of a particular bird that the chiefs had to find in the forest. A feather from this bird confirmed they had chosen the correct man to be king. I pulled out my *Birds of Eastern Africa* book and asked them to identify the bird in question.

"Was it a large bird or a small bird?" I asked.

"It is a large bird," they replied.

I opened the section on large birds and asked them to find the correct one. They thought for a minute and decided it was a Marabou Stork. I don't know if you've seen a Marabou Stork, but they are five feet high with a long straight bill and black and white feathers. I located a drawing of a Marabou and put it in the book.

A few days later, some other men were in the office and I showed them the picture of the Marabou Stork. "What?" they exclaimed. "That bird is a Marabou Stork! That's all wrong." I went into the house and brought out the bird book and asked them to identify the correct one.

"What kind of bird are we looking for? Is it a large bird?" I asked.

"Yes," they assured me. We looked through the options again and, after consideration, they decided the correct bird was a flamingo.

"A flamingo?" I asked, amazed. "You mean it has a curved beak and is pink?"

They assured me that was correct. I had never known of a flamingo coming so far north, though they are common enough in central Kenya. "Well, it is unusual to find them. That is why it is so special," they explained. So, I drew a flamingo and put the new picture in the book.

Sometime later, another of the Cøllø team looked through the book and came upon the flamingo.

"What's a flamingo doing in here?" he demanded. "The bird we are talking about is not a flamingo!" *Back to the drawing board*, I thought. I brought out the official book again and asked him to show me the bird. Finally, he admitted he couldn't show me a photo because this was a mythical bird and no one knew what it looked like. In order to preserve my sanity, we left that story without a picture.

I learned a valuable lesson. If you insist on an answer, they will give you one. It may not be the right one, but you will have an answer. So, if someone is reluctant to respond to a request, drop it.

Love,

L

Dear Harriet,

Mom traveled to Ireland, Scotland, and Wales with one of my aunts. She spent a little time in England as well and got to meet

Janice for the first time. I'm teaching again in England in early 1994, and Mom is coming to stay with me during that time. It will be great to spend time together. I'm tired, and I can't sleep enough to get rested.

Getting letters out of the country was a constant struggle. Mailing things from Sudan almost guaranteed it wouldn't reach the intended destination. So, I kept a variety of stamps from England, Kenya, and the US. People traveled, and so letters were finished hastily to get them to the intended traveler before departure. Letters coming into Sudan might or might not make it. So, we used the SIL postbox in Kenya and someone hand carried them to Khartoum.

One woman in Kenya told me her mother sent a verbal letter on a cassette tape. The tape never reached her, but as this woman shopped in a store, she heard her mother's voice over the intercom. Someone had stolen the tape from the mail and sold it to the shopkeeper. He played it, and she heard her mother's message. She convinced the manager to give her the tape!

Love,

L

Dear Harriet,

We expected twenty-five participants at the Nilotic phonology workshop. Without asking me, one of the staff invited six Nuers. We had to find a larger room to fit everyone in. I had already made the handouts, so there weren't enough. We used posters as we had no overhead projector available. I handed off three lectures to someone else, so by the start of the course, I only needed to write seven more. The course met three days per week, 4:00-6:00

p.m. We hired Onyoti to handle the logistics, and I was grateful for his help!

Three men from different language groups studied in Kenya. During a long break, they returned to Khartoum and held a meeting. The amplifiers and reverb were at full blast. They explained that languages with no writing system could be developed. The community could have cultural materials written down for future generations and they could also translate the Bible. They shouted this information to the whole of Omdurman! So much for keeping a low profile!

As a result of that meeting, we had discussions with five northern language groups asking to develop their languages, and soon had a list of fifteen more who were interested. We were already understaffed. One or two couples planned to come in 1995, but these groups would not wait that long. Everyone had far too much to do. Even I realize I can't do everything. I don't know how it will work, but I believe God wants me to watch and appreciate the miracles He will perform.

The Alphabet Storybook is ready to publish after two and a half years! It is sixty-four pages long with lots of pictures. I did the final edits on my Mac, and at first it was fun. Then it got nasty with me, and I was tempted to throw it across the room. The Mac doctors investigated the problem, but didn't have a solution. They wanted to scan pictures into the document, but I said, "Don't even mention it! I can't get it to print words, let alone pictures! How do I tell it whether it is a box or words?"

One wise guy said, "Speak loudly!" So, I shouted at my imaginary computer "You are a word and you are a box!" Now you know I'm crazy!

Love,

L

Dear Harriet,

On November 4, 1993, it will once again be illegal to hold hard currency. I have $500 left and will get rid of most of it this week and send the rest to Kenya for my travel to UK. If I put the money in the bank, it would not help me with my trip. No matter how much a person deposited, you could only take $50 out of the country. That won't get you very far. To entice people to turn in their money, they've put the bank rate up to the black-market rate. That's fine for this week, but in a few weeks, the black-market rate may continue to rise and the bank rate probably won't. Janice and I decided to purchase an air conditioner for Janice's room. Her room is so hot, you don't want to go in there during the day.

Love,

L

Dear Harriet,

I realized I should take advantage of the more historical aspects of Sudan. Several of us joined a day trip with the Archeological Society to see Jebel Moyo. It is a hill near the town of Sinnar, southeast of Khartoum. My first mistake was failing to ask about the length of the journey; the second was sitting at the back of the bus. Our vehicle was like the one I traveled on to Karima in 1982, but without the fold-down seat in the aisle. Since it was a day trip, the thirty passengers didn't need luggage. We left at 6:30 a.m. with a promise that we should reach our destination by 11:30 (five hours later). The return journey should have us back in Khartoum by 8:00 p.m.

As we traveled out of Khartoum, I realized my mistake of sitting in the rear seat. Even the small bumps in the road, which were minor events when the front wheels went over them, became major events when the rear wheels hit them. The back flew into the air, then crashed down with a jerk throwing passengers out of their seats and into the air. The driver never slowed until he came to one of the many police checkpoints. There must have been eight of these, and at each one, the officers took their time checking the paperwork. The driver did his best to make up for lost time at the expense of the backs, necks, and heads of the passengers at the back.

Since we weren't packed in, there was more room to fall. I found it helpful to hold on to the metal bar attached to the seat in front of me. I clung to it for dear life! It took several days to work the stiffness out of my hands. It was a miracle that I didn't have severe and permanent damage to my back.

Several of my companions were in an even worse location. I could brace myself using the bar on the seat ahead. The unfortunate souls in the last row had only the stairwell to the back door ahead of them. They had nothing to hold on to. In addition, the driver stored a metal box of tools under their seat. Whenever we drove over one of those bumps, the box leapt out and banged passengers on the backs of their legs before sliding back to its place. Grease and oil soon covered anything that fell to the floor. The occupants of these seats stood up for much of the trip to avoid getting a concussion. We have vowed "never again!"

When one had time to look, the countryside was interesting. The road took us through part of the Gezira Scheme, which is an agricultural area. In the past, there had not been adequate water for farming. Then they built the Roseires Dam along with a "2,700-mile (4,300-km) network of canals and ditches to irrigate fields growing cotton and other cash crops." (https://www.britannica.com/

topic/Gezira-Scheme.) It is now the most highly productive region in the country. We saw the tops of fishing boat sails moving along the canal across the hills of dirt that acted as a dike.

At 12:30, we arrived at Jebel Moyo which was an ideal time of day for getting out into the blistering sun and hiking up a small mountain. We gathered up our cameras, water bottles, and food before trekking up the hill. The *jebel* or hill itself was not very high. But for a country as flat as Sudan, it was noticeable. The shapes of the hills in that area were fascinating. One of them looked as if it had been sliced in two with a knife and half removed. (I suggested the English had shipped it to the British Museum in London. But the Brits among us didn't think they had seen it there.)

Before one of the World Wars, the British discovered the ruins we came all this way to see. They loaded the interesting remains on a ship headed to London for study and documentation. Unfortunately, the ship sank. Now we will never know who these people were or how they lived. We found a large room made of enormous stones, resembling a castle that would provide good protection. There were several structures that looked like large beehives. (These turned out to be ovens for baking bread.)

The fortress at Jebel Moyo

241

An ancient oven

The local children hung about asking for handouts and impeding the serious bird-spotters. We returned to the bus and ate lunch as we reckoned (correctly) that we would not have time to stop on the way back. If it took six hours to arrive, it would take the same time to return, especially traveling in the dark. We had taken one "comfort stop" on the way, found no facilities at Jebel Moyo, and stopped once near some bushes on the return trip. Such were the amenities.

It was after 9:00 p.m. when we reached Khartoum. I'm glad I did it once, but "never again!" will I sit in the BACK of the bus! Now you may understand why I prefer to stay at home and work.

Love,

L

Dear Harriet,

When I'm alone, I sense God's friendship and closeness filling the empty times and providing that companionship, so I don't feel lonely. It's the only way I survive. Besides, with all my faults, only a perfect God with infinite grace would put up with me, and I get the benefit of having the "perfect husband."

I met with the Bible Society consultant several times as we are trying to get the Cøllø translation started.

The Alphabet Storybook is going to press. We made twenty test copies for general inspection. Then we produced several hundred after errors had been corrected! The guys have reviewed it ten or eleven times. I want them to do an interlinear translation as it will provide good data for the paper Cathy and I are writing and add many words to the dictionary.

One of my supporting churches in Knoxville decided to sponsor Kathy to visit me for two weeks. She works in the Mission Department at the church, and after reading my letter, decided she should come to help me. She is planning to come on October 17-24, depending on the visa. I'm hoping Mom will send goodies with her. I wonder how she will cope with the heat and dust.

The Phonology workshop is going well. Very few people have missed any lectures. There are twenty-nine men and one woman. Three of our staff traveled to Nairobi for meetings, so someone from Nairobi wanted to come help, but she didn't receive a visa. I'm glad I scheduled a weeklong break. We are tired and find it difficult to work in 100°F heat. So, we are relaxing and processing what we have learned. We start back on October 4 and finish November 4. I've taught through lesson nine and have written lectures through thirteen. This week's break should provide an opportunity to complete the remaining lectures.

I just wrote you on a Kenya air form as it looked as if the next mail was heading in that direction. Turns out, they plan to stop off in Ethiopia for a week on the way. However, someone else is traveling to the US on Tuesday, so I will send this with them.

Love,

L

Dear Harriet,

It is October 3. Janice and I are sitting by the pool with the temperatures over 100°F. We've been through a jug of juice, had a swim, and eaten lunch. Now I'm trying to write a letter or two before the prayer meeting and church. Someone flies to the UK on Monday. Janice is gradually settling in, but it is so hot that she is finding it saps her energy. Also, she was running around in England and needs to rest before starting on the rigorous schedule we keep here.

When we arrived home from church, men with a pickup and ladder were pulling up to a large transformer nearby. We had power, but I said, "Prepare for blackout." Sure enough, ten minutes later... It is SO hot. At least I have a solar fan and lights. The workers are still there, so there's hope the power will return. One family across town has been without electricity for thirty hours. In 100° heat, that is not fun!

I'm planning to go to England on January 3 for the course that starts on the 10th and lasts until March 25. Janice and I are working on how to overlap and take a vacation together, but plans are still fuzzy. It will be Easter break and it may be hard to get a booking. Mom is joining me for all or part of my time in England.

The government closed the office that signs letters for our visas so none of us can leave and no new people can come. We need to find another sponsor soon! The timing was interesting. The people who needed to travel had their papers when the office closed, so they went. No one needs a stay visa until December. It is clear that Satan can attack, but God is in control!

It promises to be a busy week. The phonology course starts up again. We will attend the half-day of prayer and a workshop planning meeting. In addition, I'm working with the guys to plan their final phonology presentation. Janice plans to work on the primer. The A-Team needs me to do some keyboarding. Whew!

Love,

L

Dear Harriet,

On October 7, I turned the calendar from September to October. My eyes fell on the 18th, Mom and Dad's anniversary. I thought about the feeling of loss that both Mom and I will experience. I think I've cried more lately than I did last year. Maybe I know the pain has lessened to the point I can risk feeling my grief. I'm sure it is normal and is a process I need to go through.

Another bizarre incident happened this week. There was no fuel available. The government ran out of money. Reportedly, tankers are sitting off Port Sudan waiting to off-load the shipments when someone comes up with the $. The government supposedly told Shell Oil that they had no hard currency, so Shell should buy US dollars on the black market. We are wondering how to sign up for that exchange. Since July, the rate has gone from £s275/$1 to

£s310/$1. With this "Shell" thing, it could go higher. What happens when a country goes broke? We may soon see.

The Cølløs are teaching in a workshop, and Janice has them working on the primer. They are busy, but they enjoy the challenges and opportunities to increase their skills.

After the no fuel week, we used some of our reserves. We moved the start time of the Phonology workshop up to 3:00 so participants could get home. The attendance is still very good. We got a three-gallon allotment this week at $1.50/gallon. They say they are going to raise it to $2.00/gallon but are hesitant to do that as people are angry about not getting any fuel last week.

I've been so busy I haven't even been able to write things on my to-do list, let alone look at what was on it. Still, I can see progress and Janice is back to work. That always helps me.

Love,

L

———

Dear Harriet,

It helps to get a good night's sleep, but at 3:30 this morning, the air cooler motor blew up. There was fire and smoke. We bought a new Saudi cooler for $95. The next day, the water pump died, so I sweated through the night. Thankfully, nights are becoming cooler in mid-October. Is winter coming?

The Sudanese fear winter. They say, "People die when it gets cold." They don't own warm clothes or have enough food. So, without blankets and shelter, they become sick and die.

As the Linguistic Coordinator, I've been responding to people's monthly reports. The Technical Studies Department should be supervising language learning, but hasn't been. Two people are studying Arabic and two more are learning other languages in Kenya. Additionally, I've commented on a Phonology Statement. That was a six-page response. Another team needed help in organizing a work plan. There is no time to be bored.

At the end of the phonology workshop, each team gave both a verbal and written report of what they had learned. I asked the Cølløs to go first because I could help them. When they had misunderstood something, I reviewed that part. They prepared their presentation, but didn't want me to see it. They chose the member with the worst English to begin and the newest attendee to finish reporting. We couldn't understand what the first one said, and the second hadn't understood anything. It was a disappointment. However, in the following week during a teacher briefing, they explained everything correctly.

We had a music practice at our house on Saturday. Afterwards, we watched *Beauty and the Beast*. We ate cheese and crackers and escaped for a while. After it was over, I closed the cover of the TV and said, "The window to the outside world is now closing!"

Someone asked, "Can't we open it up again?"

Love,

L

Dear Harriet,

Next week is going to be one of THOSE weeks. We have our usual Monday trip to get the fuel. The ration is currently three gallons/week at £s400/gallon. Rumor has it that it will soon go to £s700. Tuesday, we are to attend a literacy planning meeting at 9:00, followed by a planning meeting for the editing workshop at

10:00. The phonology workshop will finish on Thursday. But we still have presentations 3:00-5:00 Monday and Tuesday with the closing ceremony on Thursday, 4:00-6:00. Wednesday is the half-day of prayer and potluck lunch followed by another meeting about the next writer's workshop, 2:00-4:00. Somewhere Janice needs to fit in time with John H to plan the content for the curriculum and evaluation workshop which runs the following week. Friday we have a Cøllø committee meeting. John H is to meet with the "other" languages on Friday afternoon, and I ought to attend. Saturday, we have a staff meeting with the Cølløs. It makes me tired just thinking about it.

A Murle pastor came from Malakal with the news that relapsing fever, typhoid, and cholera were rampant there. The government is not paying salaries, so no one can afford to buy food. We gave him a significant amount of the famine relief money to take back to help people.

My body says, "It is time to stop." I've dropped a few of my extra duties to get more rest. But the more I sleep, the more I need to sleep. If I'm sitting still at 11:00 a.m., I'm asleep. Other symptoms include indigestion and frequent burping. We had rich food over Thanksgiving, so maybe things will calm down now I'm back on my regular diet. The water in the pool is too cold for me to swim, and I haven't set up an alternative exercise program yet. How do I squeeze that into the schedule?

Love,

L

Dear Harriet,

During November, we sponsored a workshop with the Ministry of Health about HIV/AIDS. The Ministry wanted posters about this subject for several southern languages. We offered another workshop on word processing for computers and yet another on editing. The Khartoum Workshop Program has become known across Africa and throughout the SIL world.

We published a book called *Selfishness Kills*. It contained several Cøllø folktales from a previous writer's workshop. We also worked on the 1994 calendar, with the focus on the kingship and the significant plants and animals used by the king. For example, the king carries a flyswatter (a symbol of authority) made of the giraffe's tail.

Speaking of the king, we met him together with members of the Cøllø Language Oversight Committee. We waited while he met with government officials. During that time, they served us cold water and Pepsi. Afterwards, they gave us fruit juice. The king had worked in a bank before his coronation. He is well educated and appreciates our work. He said, "If you had chosen to go to the moon, it would have cost a lot of money, and would not have benefited many people. But you chose to work with the Cøllø, and many have benefited." It is not often that we hear this affirmation.

Our proposals netted $25,000 from the Ford Foundation to pay for the materials that we wanted for the Cøllø people. That money enabled us to print 3000 copies of the first third of the primer.

The Cøllø Old Testament translation work started on December 15. The guys were excited and so am I.

Love,

L

Dear Harriet,

Kathy worked as the mission secretary at one of my supporting churches. When she opened my letter in September 1993 describing the many hardships and challenges I faced, she burst into the director's office and said, "I want to go. I want to go work with Leoma." She began raising support to pay for this trip and it quickly came in. She applied for a visa to Sudan, assuming it would come quickly. But that didn't happen. Kathy had a long wait for her visa. Relations between the US and Sudan were at a low point.

Finally, in early December, the visa arrived. Within a couple of days, Kathy boarded a plane for the first time in her life and flew to Sudan via Frankfurt, Germany. In Frankfurt, she feared missing her flight, so she sat at the gate the entire time. She didn't even risk going to the bathroom! As she got off the plane in Khartoum, she saw ten to twelve soldiers with Ak47s watching each person walking down the steps. As the only American, she felt vulnerable. It was 11:05 Saturday night. She hadn't slept for two days.

I had given her a detailed map of the airport showing where to go in the required order. She also had instructions on what to say and what not to say. There were currency declaration, customs, and endless papers to complete before she emerged, with great relief, from the airport and in to my care. We climbed into the Suzuki and bumped home over the rough roads.

We didn't have a guest room, so we set up a bed and mosquito net in the sitting room. It gave little privacy, but it was the best we could do. The call to prayer awoke her at 4:30 a.m., but she soon fell asleep again. She noted in her journal, "I feel great peace knowing I am exactly where I should be, doing what I am supposed to be doing."

Janice setting up the mosquito net for Kathy (Credit: Kathy Smith)

On Sunday, we attended our group prayer meeting. There she met the rest of the team and realized each of us was tired. The reality of our prayers for our colleagues and each other touched her deeply. Along with the mail, the folks in Nairobi had sent up a crate of eggs. We divided them up after the prayer time. Then we went on to the International Church service, where different nationalities sang Christmas songs in their languages. One of the most impressive groups was the Koreans, in full Korean dress. They have the only air-conditioned church in the city! We joined to sing *Let There Be Peace On Earth* at the end.

The work that we needed done included organizing our files and keyboarding. Kathy worked hard to complete these jobs. She shared our bean breakfast with the Cølløs, learning to eat with her right hand. Mail came up from Nairobi, and she became angry that so many people had written the names of churches or something inappropriate on the envelope. (I tried to discourage that when I spoke at home because the government sees those things.) Keeping a low profile in such an environment is important.

It didn't take long for her to notice the water filter and its importance. Water cuts happened too often, and the toilet didn't always flush. Fuel rationing was a shock, as we got two gallons a week for the car. The market was not in any way similar to a grocery store.

During her stay, we had many visitors, and people invited us out as well. A Sudanese family asked us to come to their home for lunch. They lived in a mud and grass structure. Kathy hesitated to eat the food as there were many flies, but wanting to be a polite guest, she ate it. The Sudanese are so hospitable. We took Kathy to a school in the displaced area of the city. These children met under a grass shelter and were proud to be in school. As we approached, they were singing, and Kathy thought it was the most beautiful sound she had ever heard.

Children at the primary school we visited

Christmas was approaching, and Kathy couldn't help comparing what she knew was going on in Knoxville, Tennessee, and the very different activities in Khartoum. Once she arrived back home, she cried when she saw the Christmas decorations in the church. The cost of them would have fed a Sudanese family for a month. The contrast was too great, and she shed many tears. On Monday after she returned, the staff at the church asked her to share for ten minutes about her trip. She refused to say anything. "How could anyone explain such a life-changing experience in ten minutes!"

Love,

L

Chapter 7:
1994

Dear Harriet,

Janice wanted a new computer, and she wanted to buy it in the US. Since we would both be in England in 1994, and Mom is coming to England, she can bring it. She didn't need to declare it since Janice planned to take it out of the UK to Sudan.

Mom brought it as a hand carry. A customs official approached her before she got her luggage off the belt. He asked if she had a computer. She told him, "Yes. This is a computer."

"Who does it belong to?"

"It's mine, and my daughter is going to teach me how to use it." She had paid for it and Janice had not yet paid her back, so it was hers.

"What does your daughter do here?" he asked.

"I have no idea!"

He admitted defeat and let her go on through the "Nothing to declare" zone.

Love,

L

Dear Harriet,

In Sudan, I worked Monday through Thursday, Friday was off, I worked Saturday, and I had Sunday off. When I got to England, my teaching schedule changed from Monday through Friday. After a few weeks of working five straight days, my body objected. I was in class when I felt one side of my body going numb. That frightened me. A student brought me a glass of water while I sat down. I left my students working on an assignment and returned to my apartment. We phoned the local doctor for an appointment that day.

After questioning and examining me, the doctor prescribed some tablets to calm me down. He also recommended I should: (1) get enough sleep, (2) exercise at least twenty minutes three times a week, and (3) take one day off each week to get away from work. That third recommendation sounded familiar, as in "rest on the Sabbath." I had been running on adrenaline for so long, I needed to stop. Catching up meant sleeping eighteen to twenty hours a day for weeks. I think I taught my class and attended a few meetings, but otherwise, I was asleep. My mom took great care of me except for the day she made me a sandwich with both Marmite and Branston Pickle on it. Disgusting!

We made a few trips during the two months she spent with me. We traveled to Bristol, Fingest, and Marlow, as well as taking trips into London to visit friends and attend church.

I was coming around before she left, so hopefully she wasn't too worried about me. It was not an auspicious beginning to 1994. I confessed I'd pushed myself much too hard and that if I wanted to keep going for the long haul, I would have to pace myself better in the future. That goal is easier said than done, but at least it is a start.

Love,

L

Dear Harriet,

Janice and I had a week of transition, while we took a week's holiday in Cornwall. She told me what she'd been doing, so I knew where to pick up when I got back. She will teach on the literacy course in England and spend time with her mother, who is 87.

Janice with her mother

After England, I traveled to Nairobi to do my Branch Linguistic Coordinator work. A friend, Margaret, and I went to Hemmingway's on the Kenya coast. We had a restful time enjoying seafood, nice pools, shady walks on the beach, and viewing coral reefs. It was just what I needed as part of my recovery.

Our return to Nairobi was not so relaxing. We left from the Malindi Airport to fly to Mombasa. As we landed, we sat on the tarmac, not moving, not going to the gate. We continued to sit there, and I wondered, *Don't other planes need to use this runway?* We learned that on takeoff from Malindi, we lost the hydraulic fluid from the front landing gear. The front wheel would not move, and a truck had to tow us off the runway. We arrived in Mombasa at 11:30 a.m. We couldn't fly on to Nairobi as our plane was inoperable. Many passengers had international connections, so they were given first priority. By 4:00 p.m., I asked to use the airport phone to contact the SIL office in Nairobi to let them know where we were. I had the wrong number. So, I phoned the travel agent that had booked this holiday. They contacted the office in a rare three-way conversation. Long-distance calls were difficult in Kenya, and while waiting, I met a pilot, copilot, one stewardess, and the air traffic controller. He was doing everything he could to get passengers on to flights. After my call, I spoke to the controller and said I would pray for him. He responded, "Thank you."

Margaret and I sat around for another hour. A man approached us and said he wanted to help us. We thanked him. He took us to find our luggage and then told us to wait. He returned in a few minutes with our boarding passes. We settled on a plane headed to Nairobi. Every seat was taken, but the air traffic controller got on to make sure no seat was empty. He stood just in front of my seat, so I tapped him on the arm. When he turned around, it was my turn to say, "Thank you."

Love,

L

Dear Harriet,

At the intermediate writer's workshop, four Cølløs produced a news sheet called "Cïjø" (encouragement). The idea caught on like a house afire! Now that they have produced one, they can hardly contain themselves until they can make another. "The next one is going to be so much better!" People wanted to have sections for health, the translation, women's news, and to advertise the latest Cøllø book for sale. The king could send news now and then.

Meanwhile, the Cøllø translators attended a workshop on poetry and songs. The goal is to write music in their own style and examine how they create poetry. This information should make translating the Psalms much easier.

The teachers were involved in an intermediate writer's course in May, and then in June, plan to teach an introductory writer's course in Cøllø in Renk! This will be the first workshop of its kind where they are totally responsible for everything.

One Sunday, after the Cøllø service, a doctor approached me. He had opposed the new spelling system. He explained that after reading our recent books, he understood why we had changed the spelling. "Before, you had to guess what the words were by the context. Now you can really read." He had not attended any courses but could see the value of the changes. He now agrees with what we are doing. After five years, it is encouraging to see our efforts are producing results and acceptance. The committee is contributing to the project and encouraging the community to do likewise. They told people, "Why should foreigners give money for us to make books and teach classes if the community itself is not willing to contribute?"

I'll return to Kenya for our group conference in June. We keep looking for a visa sponsor.

Love,

L

Dear Harriet,

The government enacted Islamization and Arabization during this time. The Christian Herald, 12 March 1994, reported,

"Women must be veiled and dressed in black. (The daughter of a Christian minister was flogged for wearing an African dress which reached only to knee-level.) All schools and universities must now teach in Arabic instead of English. This includes private school and church schools. Students who wish to go on to higher studies must pass an exam in Islamic Religion... Some soldiers have reported receiving salary bonuses for impregnating females among the Nuba people and southerners. The aim is to produce an ethnically mixed and Muslim new generation.

"In 1991-1992, hundreds of thousands of refugees from the South, who were living in shanty towns around Khartoum, were evicted by government forces. Their homes were bull-dozed. They were taken to various sites in the desert around Khartoum, and left there without food, shelter or water.

"The government gave relief help only to Muslims and those willing to convert to Islam. One Sudanese church leader declared: 'We would rather die with Christ than become Muslims with food.

"Western intelligence has recently confirmed that Sudan, under the tutelage of Iran, is playing a key role in promot-ing Islamic terrorism around the world. Training camps in Sudan are used to teach the techniques of terrorism to fun-damentalists from Saudi Arabia, Egypt, Algeria, Morocco, Tunisia and even Uganda. In August 1993, the American government added Sudan to its list of nations sponsoring terrorism."

An Islamic conference was held around this time, and when they departed, they left a lot of spiritual baggage behind. They held this conference near my house, and I felt the effects of it, especially when I was alone. I had panic attacks, depression, and a deep-seated fear that if I did a particular thing like take an aspirin, I would die. It was quite unnerving. I asked my colleagues to pray with me and for me. The heaviness would lift for a time, but then return.

Love,

L

Dear Harriet,

Back in November 1993, three groups in the north of Sudan asked us to help them develop their languages. When I returned from England, I learned that there were no longer three languages, but fifteen! While I was away, they had announced they were ready to meet us on Thursday afternoons from 4:00-6:00. John H got them to produce a word list. Each week, he gave them assignments. They should return the next week with it completed. When I arrived, he handed them on to me. These languages are not dialects. They come from three to four sub-families, which means there are similarities but many differences. Temperatures in the afternoon when we meet are often 115°F in the shade. The rooms where we meet have fans and lights which work if the power is on. Each group must pay $.50 each month to give us a soda each week. They decided that, not us.

I wish you could see their enthusiasm. It just amazes me every week. First, I help them learn their vowels. Arabic only has three vowels, so those schooled in Arabic are only aware of those. Their own language may have eight to ten. To find the vowels, they beat out the word, as in sy-la-ble. That word has three beats, and thus three vowels. Once they know how many vowels are in the word, they need to figure out what vowels are there. They list words with the same vowel letters and listen if they sound the same or different. They do well with words like "see" versus "soon," but not so well on "feet" versus "fit," "suit" and "soot," or "caught" and "cot." If there is a bright member in the group who "gets it," she or he helps the others.

One participant is the Dean of the Physical Education Department at the University of Khartoum. He always comes late and asks a million wonderful questions. I would like to take him aside and give him a course in phonetics and phonology and then let him teach.

We want them to concentrate on their vowels while we are away in June. In July, we'll see what sounds they have and what letters they want to use. Then we can get computers set up for trial editions of alphabet books in October and November. None of these groups have any funds, but the Ford Foundation is eager to give them money once they write a proposal.

Love,

L

Dear Harriet,

When I returned to Khartoum in April, my desk was piled high with work. The desk is three feet from my bed, so even if I lie down, I still see the work and feel the urge to get up and DO something. After much prayer, I visited the acting landlady. "Could we use the large storage room in the house for an office? I need to get my desk out of my bedroom." Within days, she agreed that if I cleared out the extra rooms, we could use them.

Once we got into the room, we found tables, chairs, china, cupboards, and a cooker (stove and oven). We sold most of the furniture and sent the money to the landlady. There was an amazing collection of old pans, dishes, pitchers, grinding mills, mattresses, pillows, blankets, clothes, shoes, tires, inner tubes, and a car door. The list could fill a whole page. We expected someone could make use of them, so we held a yard sale for the Cølløs. Our staff priced the things, then had the first choice to buy it.

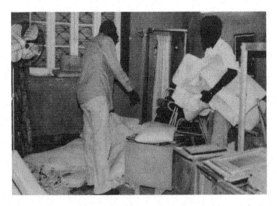

Inner room being cleaned out

Tire inner-tubes

We gave the money raised to Operation Mercy to help the people displaced from their homes and now out in the desert. Once the stuff was gone, we rewired the room, painted it, and turned it into my bedroom, a private sitting room, and a dining room. My old bedroom became the office.

Love

L

Dear Harriet,

The Cøllø teachers traveled to a village called Wada Kona, south of Renk, to run their first ever writer's workshop in the Cøllø language. We taught workshops only in English. The language of instruction limited who could attend. None of us knew how to run one in Arabic or which version of Arabic to use. It took years before the Sudanese taught workshops in Arabic. This, however, was the first workshop to be taught in the mother tongue, and it was exciting.

The Cøllø team hoped to have twenty participants in the workshop. They planned three weeks for the course, working four days per week from 7:15-1:30. The goal for the workshop included teaching the material and getting the participants to write stories. Peter M planned to type the stories in book format on stencils using a manual typewriter. He put five of the stories into book form to give to each participant for the closing of the course. He reproduced the books by putting the stencils on a silkscreen duplicator since there was no electricity there. At the closing ceremony, each participant received a copy of the book along with a certificate of completion. It was a magnificent goal.

Silkscreen equipment

The morning before their departure, they realized they needed an official letter sanctioning their meetings. We drafted a letter and got it signed and stamped. They also needed letters requesting the participants be excused from work. We printed out twenty of these and had them signed and stamped. If a document isn't stamped, no one takes it seriously.

They left with £s125,000, books, lecture notes, handouts, a typewriter, stencils, pens, paper, a long-armed stapler and staples, and certificates. As they loaded up to go to the bus, their clothes took up very little space. The vehicle groaned under the boxes of books, a 50 lb. sack of sugar, lentils, tea, chalk, etc., and a mattress that Peter M is taking to his family. Our goal to make them independent was happening. I felt as if I'd sent the guys off to college!

Early in the morning, they headed to the bus station for the two-day trip to Renk and on to Wada Kona. There were no phones, so we had to wait, pray, and hope things were going well.

I won't keep you in suspense as long as we were. It went brilliantly! The team returned with glowing reports of their success. They had thirteen participants who attended faithfully. The teachers were excited that the lectures presented in their own language were so much clearer and understandable. The participants received the books at the closing ceremony, along with the participation certificates. They included pictures and a cover. Once back in Khartoum, Peter M keyboarded them into the computer and we printed them in a more finished form. The teachers were thrilled and so were we. The Cøllø literacy project was moving from success to success.

Love,

L

Dear Harriet,

Our visa situation remained problematic. Four governors met with a minister in the government and they all agreed we had to stay. So, Richard, our Sudanese administrative assistant, visited the Security Office to find out what the holdup was. He explained he had to report the issue to the Vice President and ten state governors at a meeting. The security officer said, "Oh, there's no problem. Come on Monday and we'll have them ready for you!" There's been a problem for three weeks; now there's no problem. I reckon God is on the move again.

I'm still battling with a fear of dying or contracting a dreaded disease. As soon as I pray, especially with someone, it goes away. But there have been some ferocious bouts of late. The enemy is attacking, and I claim Christ's power, but I have to keep doing it.

I'm grieving for Dad; I miss his letters. Also, my friend Amos had a heart attack, the second in three years. That brought back many memories. At least I'm getting more sleep and exercising regularly. I call myself a "recovering workaholic."

Love,

L

Dear Harriet,

Cathy and I worked on a linguistic paper about Cøllø grammar for a month. We worked with the guys to collect data on Tuesdays and Thursdays. Cathy's expertise is in grammar and mine is phonology and hearing the sounds. It takes both of us to do this. Once we had the data, I entered it into the computer, and that took hours. I had to include all the tones and vowel lengths besides the English meaning. Then we examined the data to find the patterns. On July 19, we had a breakthrough because of Otto, one of the translators and a brilliant natural linguist. We kept hearing a vowel that was there and then wasn't there, depending on the meaning of the sentence. Otto mentioned one of these vowels was long or stressed. Suddenly, things slotted into place. I explained our theory to them and how to write it, and they agreed. We need to get this defined because it will have implications for the primer. Once we saw it and understood the differences in meaning, it was so simple (a sign it is probably real). We were excited and overjoyed!

Let me give you a bit of an example. I'll use the word for "burn" *räb*. The verb can be changed in fifty-five different ways. Most of the changes involve only a change of the vowel, but adding an extra "b" at the end, as in *räbba*, changes the meaning. The tone of the vowels can also change, and various vowels can be before and after the word. Meaning changes are:

- Bill used to burn grass all the time and still does.
- I'm surprised that Bill used to burn grass because he doesn't do it anymore.
- I heard that Bill burned grass, but I didn't see him do it.
- Bill was burned (possibly by the grass).

And there are plenty more where those came from.

Love,

L

———

Dear Harriet,

Over the years, the Cøllø Language Oversight Committee and teachers had agreed to significant changes in the spelling system and the alphabet. But the community in the home area had not given input to these decisions. The project leader selected a team of teachers to go to Malakal to connect with the important leaders and conduct a one-week workshop. We discussed strategies for dealing with contentious issues, hopefully leading to a successful resolution. I suggested they present related topics each day and then have the attendees break up into small groups for discussion. At the end of the small group session, they should come back and share their conclusions. By the end, we hoped most everyone would agree.

This strategy appealed, as they like everyone to have their say. So, off they went to Malakal. Once they arrived, they explained the purpose of their visit. The elders were indignant that they had not been involved from the beginning. Our team faced an uphill battle.

The bishop of the Catholic Church offered his video camera to document at least parts of the meeting. They only filmed the first and last days since the battery was weak. My, what a contrast!

They held the meetings in a large government building with guards posted at the doors to make sure only invited guests entered. The participants arrived with their folders and papers, ready to engage with the topic. The team used their time well. They presented the history of how the writing system developed, going through the various changes and additions through eighty years. Then they got to the specifics. They explained the problems we were trying to resolve, and the options suggested. Anyone with counter suggestions had time to present their ideas. Then the small groups evaluated the options and made their decision. There was usually consensus when the groups came back together to report.

The video clips from the first day showed the chairman of the Malakal Council looking irritated and offended. The participants sat with arms folded and angry looks on their faces. Five days later, the video showed a drastic change of mood. The smiling chairman gave a speech supporting the work done in Khartoum and expressing his appreciation for the team. The participants looked jovial and satisfied. They accepted all our proposed changes. It was a miracle!

A few people disagreed and fought to turn back the tide. However, the community had spoken. From that day onward, whenever someone suggested going back to the "old orthography," people shouted them down. "We don't want to go back to the old way." For the first time, I believed our success was possible. With the community behind the work, my efforts would not fade away. The Cøllø implemented the changes because they found them useful and important.

Love,

L

Dear Harriet,

Janice and I began to hand over literacy work to the Cølløs. We had spent years training people, and they showed initiative and ability.

The committee was taking more interest, so it seemed like a good time. They should run things since it was their language.

We had a sub-committee meeting to discuss how to restructure the office, with the men officially taking up responsible positions. They are doing the jobs, but have been in training. They would need us for a time, but we felt they'd reached the point of doing everything themselves. The men understood, but the committee needed to look at their role as well.

We had a meeting about adding tone marks as it was popping up all over the place. Tone shouldn't be marked on every word. But when there is a difference between a singular and a plural, tone marking would help. Tone is also crucial in verbs. While they saw the need, they didn't know how to explain it to people. One of them said, "If we didn't have the English meaning here, we wouldn't know what it meant." They saw the importance, but couldn't defend it if people asked questions. The primer is to be printed in October, so we have a month to let them think about it.

As Janice and I planned our exit from this project, we needed to establish who would run the office. We held a different opinion from the committee. In the end, the committee appointed a succession of people into leadership. None of them read or wrote Cøllø, had no teaching experience, and did not understand how the project operated. They expected a big salary, but this was a voluntary position. A few committee members and the new leadership thought there was money and wanted access to it. Unfortunately, our generous funding sources had moved on to other projects and were unwilling to continue supporting literacy in Sudan. Try as we might, we could not connect with the new leadership. We offered further training, but they never caught the vision of how to move forward. It is said, "When the owner leaves the work, it dies." I guess we still owned too much and maybe departed too soon.

With increasing demands from other language groups, we needed to turn loose of something. We released the Cølløs. It proved a painful time for everyone, and a hard learning experience.

Love,

L

Dear Harriet,

In June, we had our branch conference. Peter K came from the UK as our guest speaker for our spiritual retreat. One evening, I shared my feelings of fear, depression, and anxiety. I believed these attacks resulted from the Islamic conference held in Khartoum. He listened, and at the end of my story, thoughtfully said, "I don't know how you will feel about what I'm going to say, but I can tell you it works for me."

Intrigued, I asked him to continue. He said, "When I am under spiritual attack, I like to go out into a field alone. Then I focus my mind on God and speak in tongues. I believe that God enables us to say things we don't know how to say to the Enemy. When we speak aloud, the Enemy hears us and flees."

That was an unexpected answer! I have had negative experiences with people who believed the gift of tongues was the only true sign of a Christ-follower. On the other hand, I was desperate. The next evening before the service, I had a terrible headache, for which I took a Tylenol and an aspirin together. A voice in my head said, "If you take that aspirin, you will die!" I decided to take it. I led the worship time, and as we sang, the voice emphasized I was going to die. So, while everyone else was singing, I was speaking in tongues. The voice stopped. Over the coming weeks and months, I used Peter's advice, and the Enemy stopped bothering me.

Love,

L

Dear Harriet,

As Cathy and I were completing our paper, I had a sinus infection. I wanted to spend more time in bed to get rid of the fever. But in twenty-four hours, we had fifty people come to the house. I haven't had time for a nap for two days. But tomorrow, Cathy leaves for the US and my pillow and I will become better acquainted!

I postponed my tone workshop since there is no one to assist me. I'm tired and don't have all the information I need to finish the lectures. So, it won't happen until October at the earliest. That's a relief.

One Friday, we went along to a celebration for the completion of the Murle New Testament and Genesis. We had prayed for that project for two years. Everyone gathered in a compound with a mud house, mud floor, and mud walls. The leader of the translation checking team has tuberculosis. In his speech, he said, "We have so much. God has blessed us with so many blessings, and now we will have the New Testament as well. We can only thank God." That was a humbling experience.

Love,

L

Dear Harriet,

In August, French authorities learned that Carlos the Jackal had entered Sudan under a false name with a diplomatic passport. Carlos was a mythical figure blamed for a string of bombings and killings across Western Europe in the 1970s and 1980s. His real name is Ilich Ramirez Sanchez, and he is from Venezuela. The French, along with intelligence agencies from several Western countries, have been on his trail for twenty years. He spent many years in Damascus, Syria, living off his reputation and drinking heavily. French intelligence officers tipped off the Sudanese authorities, and after the Sudanese checked him out, they arrested him and sent him to France. The Sudanese officials wanted to improve their international image. "It is part of our moral conviction to fight against this kind of activity," a government spokesman said in London. "The government of Sudan in doing this is fulfilling its obligations to the international community in fighting terrorism and fighting against terrorists." (*The Chattanooga Times*, August 16, 1994, A3.)

Many of us felt we were under attack. One Sudanese colleague's father was arrested for having a shortwave radio and a few medicines for his family. He has worked as a medical assistant for thirty years. They held him in a 12x12 room with 60 others. There was one small window, so little circulation. The temperatures were well over 100°F. They had to take turns sitting down, and it was very difficult to breathe. They released him after two to three days on £s1,000,000 bail! No charges were brought, but he still had to go to court.

In the same week, we heard the police brought a lorry full of street children to the police station and left them sitting in the sun for hours. Then the police beat the children with belts.

One of my American colleagues got picked up by the security police and put in an unmarked car. They drove him around from security post to security post. He saw weapons on the floorboard of the vehicle. The one who picked him up became confused, as no one wanted to take responsibility for him. So, they released him. Maybe God confused them. These instances happened in one week's time.

Love,

L

Dear Harriet,

Our ancient video player bit the dust. We asked our neighbor, Chris, if she would go in with us to buy a new VCR and TV. She agreed, but none of us had enough money. So, we contacted yet another friend, Colin, who was coming back from England to ask if he would bring extra money. He obliged, and on the eventful day, the four of us headed to the out-of-the-airport Duty Free. It was hot and humid, and the air conditioning was broken. The management set up a huge air cooler to relieve the heat, but only made it more humid. Now and then, we took a break to stand in front of air coming from the cooler to tolerate being in the building for a few more minutes.

Janice, Chris, and I raced around, trying to find the largest TV and the nicest VCR for the money available. We examined twenty different TV sets to ensure compatibility with the VCR we had selected. It took forty-five minutes to make our decision, and then it was time to pay.

We headed to the declaration form desk with our four currency declarations, cash dollars, cash pounds sterling, and dollar traveler's checks. When the cashier saw that, he refused. We had to have all the money on one form. After serious negotiations, Colin convinced the man that none of us had enough money on our own. In the end, the man relented and agreed to allow multiple forms. I doubt he would have made such a generous concession for us women, but for Colin, he agreed. I guess that was a man thing. He struggled to make sure we paid him the correct amount since there were two types of currency: dollars and pounds. The counting process took one and a half hours. After an eternity, we completed the sale and left the "hot house" with our TV and VCR.

Once we got home, we did not know how to connect them. Colin had fled the scene as soon as we got outside the Duty Free. We got hold of someone under twenty-five years of age to hook it up and get it working. We enjoyed using this setup for many years. The video player moves between houses. If Chris needs it, she takes it to her house. When we want to watch it, we bring it to ours. Thankfully, there haven't been any serious conflicts of interest yet.

Love,

L

Dear Harriet,

We finally have the extra rooms cleared out, and are making plans to fix them up. The living room part of our house used to be the verandah. They had tiled over the drains, so instead of being level, it felt like the sea. I decided to get the floor retiled. George, the contractor, had given me the estimate for the materials and the work. I told him that when everything was in the compound, he could start tearing up my floor. Every door in the house opens into that room. We have to go through it to get to the bathroom, the kitchen, the outside, and each of our bedrooms. On Monday morning, George came to start digging up our floor. I asked, "Where are the tiles? Where is the sand?"

"The tiles will be ready today."

"When they are ALL here, then and only then can you tear up my house! And what's more, once you start, no one takes a holiday, no one gets sick, and nobody dies!"

George looked at me in amazement and replied, "You've been here a long time, haven't you?"

I've seen too many instances where they start work and then they can't finish it for weeks because the materials are not available. The sand arrived on Monday, but I've yet to see the tiles.

The tiles arrived on Tuesday, so George and his crew came at 7:30 on Wednesday morning to dig up the crumbly floor. Before long, they began to remove the partition between our sitting room and the new rooms. Janice, Peter M, Roda, and I removed items from the sitting room. Pictures came down, cushions stacked up, tables unloaded, the TV and video player moved, and the bookcase shifted. In thirty minutes, the place echoed, and we marveled at how big it was with so little in it.

George promised not to start the cementing process until Thursday, as we couldn't get into either the bathroom or Janice's room once that began. Since we had to go outside to get to the kitchen or to my room, we planned to spend two nights with a friend.

After an evening out, we returned to find the living room was one big sandpile. The cats had a ball! They thought they were outside in the biggest litter box ever! We called the new décor "Picnic by the Nile." We had the atmosphere of the picnic without having to leave home. Screens on the windows and doors meant no flies or mosquitoes. And if we forget something, the kitchen is nearby.

Love,

L

Dear Harriet,

They de-rationed the fuel, so now, we can buy as much as we want for $2.25 a gallon. We also bought an air cooler for the new rooms for $500. The first one we purchased was locally made and needed frequent repairs. Our Egyptian friends told us to buy a Saudi cooler with American mats. We followed this advice and indeed, it worked much better and only occasionally needed repairs.

Visas continued to come along with residence permits. Despite the difficulties, God is keeping the way open for us to stay.

Janice left me to deal with the redecorating. She was busy with the primer. Soon, I was ready to pull my hair out and was thinking, *I want my daddy or an uncle*! It was stressful. We divided the very large salon into two rooms, one my new bedroom and the other an inner sitting room. There was a double-door-sized-hole in the wall, so I asked the carpenter, "Where's the door?"

"What door? I don't know anything about a door."

When George turned up, I asked him about it. He said, "Oh, we never planned a door there!"

"This is a sitting room and that is a bedroom! There has to be a door!"

We had a door about the right size between the inner sitting room and the new dining room. "Can we move this door?"

"Oh, yes. No problem." They took the doorframe and doors out, leaving a gaping hole. Then we saw termites had riddled both uprights. He was going to put the frame straight into the new wall, termites and all. But I said, "Oh, no you don't! Cut off the part with the termites and replace it with good wood." So, he spent hours working on it with more to do tomorrow. We painted the bottom with used motor oil to discourage the termites.

Janice and I departed for our friend's house so George and his team could place the tiles and cement them together. Peter M stayed and watched them like a hawk. He sat on a folding chair and monitored their every move. Otherwise, George or his team could have picked up anything they fancied.

Once George finished the floor, we returned. The main room needed to be painted, but we ran out of paint. The electrical wiring is incomplete. The electrician had an accident on his motorbike and can't work for two weeks. Another man will finish the job.

Love,

L

Dear Harriet,

We continued to meet with the committee and in October, it took two and a half hours to get to the second agenda item. After four hours, we reached the fourth item and things were not going well. Maybe that's part of nationalization. They no longer feel compelled to do it my way. I'm trying to distance myself as I'm being pulled toward so many other languages. Changing leadership is a tricky business. We learned the system for promotion in Sudan requires you to promote the first-hired, regardless of whether or not they can do the job.

I suggested two alternative plans. First, the committee should interview each candidate. That process would accomplish two things: (a) The committee would understand what each position involved as I would supply relevant questions, and (b) They could judge the qualifications for themselves.

The second idea was for the teachers to decide and give their proposal to the committee. It is their project, after all.

When we left the project, we met with the council at a general meeting of the Cøllø community. We thanked them for their commitment over the years, wished them well, and offered to be available upon request. I apologized for the mistakes I made without specifying them. Hopefully, they all got covered, even the ones I didn't know about.

Love,

L

Dear Harriet,

In mid-December, Wanda and I went to Ethiopia for Christmas. It was a blessing to get away from the tensions and stress of Khartoum. Thankfully, Ethiopia doesn't have the same spirit of chaos that Sudan has. Our plans were not very firm, but we arrived at the SIM guest house. They had a room waiting for us and lunch. We enjoyed hot water for baths or showers and comfortable beds. What more could you want? We relaxed, worked on a jigsaw puzzle, and watched a video. One of my Ethiopian friends from the University of London took us on a walking tour and then invited us to his home for lunch the next day.

We made our arrangements for traveling to Tulegit in the southwest part of Ethiopia near the Sudan border. My friends Mike and

Hileen worked there. We took presents: cheese, chocolate, maraschino cherries, pecans, vegetables, and fruit. After Christmas, I planned to travel up north with friends to visit the Blue Nile Falls, Lalibela, and other tourist spots.

I've taken on additional responsibilities with the Thursday Language Club. We are working with languages I've never heard of. Some want literature and education material, others want to translate the New Testament. There's never a dull moment. I'm resting regularly and leaving more undone than I used to, and my body appreciates it.

Love,

L

Dear Harriet,

My trip to see Mike and Hileen was interesting. Wanda and I flew from Addis Ababa to Tum (tomb). The small plane limited our luggage allowance. We took a few clothes, but mostly food. Once we arrived in Tum, an Ethiopian drove us to Tulegit. That trip took about three to four hours over what was supposed to be a road. It looked more like an unmarked path. We bounced over boulders, inched through creeks and plowed through eight-foot grass. At one point, we saw a local man nearby dressed in a pair of flip-flops and a necklace, carrying a bow and arrow. I kept my nose and mouth covered throughout the journey because of my severe allergies to grass.

Mike and Hileen's house looked like half an eggshell. There was a comfortable open plan living room, kitchen, dining room downstairs and bedrooms upstairs. Down the hill was the outhouse. One afternoon, I went to use the facility. As I sat on the "throne,"

I felt I was being watched. I looked behind me and saw a snake looking my way. I hastened along with my business and headed back to the house to report. Mike dealt with it while teaching his three young children about snakes.

The Surma, among whom they worked, are linguistically related to the Murle and similar groups in southern Sudan. These groups herd cattle and believe that God gave all the cattle in the world to them, but other groups stole them. They are duty bound to retrieve them. That leads to a vehement reaction from the ones who lose the cattle and respond with weapons. Gunshot wounds were not uncommon. The Surma live a simple lifestyle, herding cattle, drinking milk and blood, raising a few crops and living in grass and mud houses. They do not have salt, sugar, or oil. The only things I saw from the outside were Ak47 assault rifles and a soccer ball.

Clothing is not considered essential in this tropical climate. The men have cloths they can throw over their shoulders if it is chilly. Otherwise, they fold them and carry the cloths on their heads. The women wear skirts. A woman's value depends on how large her lip plate is. Her mother punctures her lower lip and inserts a small disk. Over time, larger disks stretch the lip until she wears a six- to eight-inch disk. She commands a high bride price if her lip doesn't split. The women don't wear the disk every day. Without it, the lower lip hangs down around her chin. What we will do for beauty!

My most indelible memory is of Christmas morning. An American missionary, Pastor John, tried to tell the story of Jesus' birth in Surma. Five or six men stood around, leaning on their spears, listening intently. As I watched them, I realized, here are thousands of people who don't even know there IS a Christmas. They do not know what it is about, or what that could mean to them. What's more, there is not yet a clear way to tell them in their own language so they can understand. My vision was renewed: This is why I'm in Sudan doing this work. We want to bring the story of God's great love to those who have never heard.

Most of the Surma don't even speak the national language, Amharic. Only one man had ever been to school. Trying to learn a language without the benefit of a common language is very challenging and takes a long time. Working with someone via Amharic is a little easier, but that depends on how well each person knows Amharic. The script is also challenging.

1st	2nd	3rd	4th	5th	6th	7th	8th
ሀ	ሁ	ሂ	ሃ	ሄ	ህ	ሆ	ሇ
[hə]	[hu]	[hi]	[ha]	[he]	[hɨ]	[ho]	[hou]
በ	ቡ	ቢ	ባ	ቤ	ብ	ቦ	ቧ
[bə]	[bu]	[bi]	[ba]	[be]	[bɨ]	[bo]	[bou]
ከ	ኩ	ኪ	ካ	ኬ	ክ	ኮ	ኯ
[kə]	[ku]	[ki]	[ka]	[ke]	[kɨ]	[ko]	[kou]

Source: https://scriptsource.org/cms/scripts/page.php?item_id=script_detail&key=Ethi

Our visit came to an end, so the question was, how do we get back to civilization? A tiny plane could take two or three people at a time. There were about six of us departing. When landing, the winds were not favorable, and the pilot wasn't sure if he could risk two trips. Wanda and I were on the second load. If the plane didn't return from the twenty-minute flight to Tum, we would have to repeat the three-hour drive. I was not eager to do that. We were excited to see the plane return to pick us up.

Instead of flying on Ethiopian Air to Addis, we took a larger mission plane back. The pilot flew us over rugged mountain ranges and fields of bright yellow *t'eff*. *T'eff* is the most commonly grown cereal grain in Ethiopia, and the one they use to make *njera*. *Njera* is like

Sudanese *kisra*, only thicker. It covers a large round tray, with spoonfuls of various dishes placed on top. You eat with your right hand, tearing off bits of *njera* and picking up bits of your preferred dish. People say it is the tastiest doormat they've ever eaten.

(More to be told in *I Can Be Lost Anywhere*, Book 4 in the Not How I Planned It series.)

Love,

L

Chapter 8:
1995

Dear Harriet,

Once I returned to Khartoum, I had a mountain of mail waiting for me. I spent days reading it, encouraged that so many people remembered me! Cathy sent a card with meditations for women who do too much. "I give thanks for my opportunities to learn, even if they don't always look like gifts at the time." And "Sometimes it helps to know that I just can't do it all."

A colleague arrived from England on January 4 and stayed with me. Janice returned January 10. Our house was now large enough to accommodate guests!

Love,

L

Dear Harriet,

Ramadan rolled around once again in February. Because the Muslims don't eat or drink from 4:30 a.m.–6:00 p.m., no one sells cooked, ready-to-eat food during the day. We buy beans the evening before to offer breakfast for our visitors and workers. We hope we have enough. So far, we have. Peter M gets bread in the morning, as it needs to be fresh. We need to have plenty because we can't predict how many hungry people will show up!

The neighborhood kids have soccer matches until midnight and men play cards until 2:00. Soon, the imam and his assistants read the Koran from 2:15 a.m. until 5:00. The boys bang drums and pots at 3:30 a.m. to wake people for "supper" before the fast begins. After losing several hours of sleep, I played a music tape to drown them out. The uplifting music kept me from losing my temper. In the morning, everyone sleeps in so shops open and transport begins later and later. At the end of this upside-down month, there is a four-day feast to celebrate the end of fasting! We stock extra food because no shop or market opens for two days.

On the positive side, we finished part 1 of the transition book. It is four months late, and only half of what I'd hoped to do, but it works! The men using it improved their spelling by the end. What encouragement! It feels good to finish something that's been on my to-do list for far too long. I'm eating a piece of chocolate to celebrate.

Love,

L

Dear Harriet,

I traveled to Moyo in northwestern Uganda on a consulting trip to study the tones in Ma'di. My travel agent explained that the Sudan Air flight goes to Kampala once a week on Friday, but comes back to Khartoum three times: Friday, Sunday, and Monday. *What?*

In typical Sudanese fashion, the plans for my trip changed three times in as many days. Plan One was to leave on February 24 on Sudan Air from Khartoum, direct to Kampala. Then I would catch a mission plane, MAF (Mission Aviation Fellowship), on the 24th or 25th to Moyo. I planned to work with my colleagues until the 29th and return to Kampala to sightsee with Wanda. She planned to attend a conference in Kampala, and would come early to tour with me. She has connections in Kampala and in Jinja, the source of the White Nile. This plan was firming up, only we didn't know if I could fly on MAF on the 24th or 25th. MAF pilots prefer to leave very early in the morning and may not fly on Saturday.

Wanda's conference was canceled. So, I changed to Plan Two: leaving on the 17th, spending the weekend in Kampala and then flying to Moyo on Monday. I would return on Thursday and fly back to Khartoum on Friday. Then everything changed again. Plan Three: the MAF flight goes at 10:00 a.m. on Friday. Sudan Air is due in at 8:00 a.m. Wanda's conference is back on and so are our travel plans. We won't know what we will actually do until it's over. This uncertainty would have driven Dad up the wall, but I thrive on it. It's just as well.

Love,

L

Dear Harriet,

By March, I felt GOOD for the first time in a year and a half. Such is the price of burnout.

My trip to Uganda proved to be an adventure. First, the travel agent told me the departure time had moved up to 3:00 a.m. So, I was at the airport by 1:00. No one had mentioned this change to the pilot, so I waited until 5:00 a.m. I couldn't always understand which flight they called, so I walked over to the exit to check. The agents sent me back to my seat saying, "Wait." Hours dragged by as the waiting lounge emptied until only two of us remained. The other passenger was a gentleman who only spoke Arabic. He asked one of the staff if the plane was going to Entebbe or not. The staff person gave the "just a minute" sign and went off to see. Moments later, the announcer called the flight. We boarded the bus to the plane. Two bags sat on the tarmac: one for him and the other for me. We identified them and climbed aboard. As the only two passengers, we nearly froze as there were no other people to warm up the air. Of course, there were no blankets.

We arrived in time for me to catch the MAF plane to Moyo. Jack met me and drove to his house where his wife, Melinda, welcomed me. We ate lunch, but having been up the entire night and much of the day, I needed a nap. I slept for a couple of hours. When I awoke, I decided to brush my teeth. I headed to the bathroom and opened my travel bag. The toothpaste seemed fuller than I remembered, but I was still groggy. As I put the toothbrush in my mouth, I felt a burning sensation. That woke me up. I looked more carefully at the toothpaste tube and discovered it was Deep Heat, an ointment for sore muscles. *Can that kill you?* I hoped not.

I helped Jack develop a system for studying the tones of the language and assisted Melinda with cooking and shopping. She was pregnant, so she appreciated the help. We had a productive five days before I returned to Entebbe. During my visit, I met a general who owned property near my friend's house. He invited me to visit him at his office when I returned to Entebbe.

Wanda's conference got canceled, so I took a few days to familiarize myself with Kampala. I stayed in a guest house that was basic, but clean, and in the middle of town. Uganda was beginning to recover after the disastrous rule of Idi Amin. Yoweri Museveni took control in 1986, and as of 2024, he is still the President of Uganda. Artists opened small shops to display their work—a good sign life is returning to normal. I paid my visit to the general's office, and he was very kind. After meeting ambassadors and kings, I realized that even generals are just people wanting acceptance and appreciation.

I had visited Kenya, Ethiopia, Sudan, and Uganda during the past few months. I found it striking that no one in Uganda complained that life was hard or expensive. Cost was an issue in all the countries I had visited, and people complained. Not the Ugandans. I asked the receptionist at the Guest House about it. She just looked at me and smiled. "Things were worse before?" I asked. She continued to smile, but said nothing.

I returned to Khartoum on one of those days that Sudan Air didn't fly from Khartoum, but only returned there. In reality, they flew first to Nairobi, Kenya, and then to Entebbe before heading to Khartoum. The Entebbe airport was new, and the janitors kept it sparklingly clean. I was impressed with the bathrooms and the waiting areas. The notice board never listed my flight, but they announced it, so I got to the right gate in time. There were more passengers on the way back to Khartoum.

Love,

L

Dear Harriet,

By mid-March, it got hot again, much to my displeasure. We had taken the motor and pump out of the air coolers at the beginning of winter to prevent them being stolen. Our maintenance men painted the coolers to prevent rust. Peter N installed the motors and pumps, turning off all the switches to keep from being electrocuted. But as he connected the wires for the motor, they sparked and he nearly got burned. He tried the next cooler, and the same thing happened. He picked up the wire to the motor and tested it. No spark. As he lifted the wire to connect it to the motor, sparks flew. He couldn't find the source of the problem, so left and sent an electrician over to have a look.

Love,

L

Dear Harriet,

By this time, I was forty-four years old. Things happen to one's body at that age, and mine developed a fibroid in my uterus. I found an excellent doctor in Khartoum. She diagnosed my problem straightaway, and put me on Progesterone to keep me from becoming anemic. She offered to operate, but I could not imagine keeping a sterile environment with all the dust. Also, my workload would make it difficult to rest.

In April, I returned home for surgery. I left within two weeks, as the doctor recommended sooner rather than later. Mom set up an appointment for me with her geriatric doctor, who referred me to the gynecologist. This same doctor had treated one of my cousins for ovarian cancer. The geriatric doctor came by to see me in the hospital, so I asked her, "What is wrong with my mother?"

Mom had not been herself, and I was concerned. So, the doctor's answer surprised me. She said, "She has dementia."

"Why do you think she has dementia?"

"She's depressed. I gave her antidepressants and she hasn't gotten better. So, it is probably dementia."

"My mother does not have dementia. There are many anti-depressants out there. Give her a different one!"

Once I recovered from surgery, I went with Mom to her next appointment. The doctor prescribed a different medication, and Mom's mental state improved. She showed no signs of dementia to the day she passed away in 2011. She was just dealing with a great deal of grief at losing my dad.

Love,

L

Dear Harriet,

While I was in the US, Janice decided to visit before starting a one-year master's degree in adult literacy. She will take the course in England so she can be near her mother.

Mom and I wanted to show Janice a good time, so we visited Nashville. A friend of ours knew someone who worked at the Opryland Hotel. He arranged tickets for us to the Grand Ole Oprey. When we collected the tickets, the agent said, "You must know someone to get these seats!" Our source worked as a parking attendant, but yes, we knew someone. We stayed at the hotel one night, then attended the show the next evening. It was great fun, as our seats were in the fifth row from the stage. Bill and Lois happened to be at the Opryland Hotel. I hadn't seen them since I left Doleib Hill in 1983. Bill was attending a conference and had a ticket to the show with his group. We included Lois with us. She laughed and said, "I don't know where Bill is sitting, but it's farther back than we are!"

We should have stayed a second night, but we drove the three hours home at midnight. On the drive, I hoped to listen to the radio to keep me awake. But the car battery had died a few weeks before our trip, and the radio couldn't be operated without a code. We did not know how to find the code, so Janice and I sang instead. I think Mom was in the back seat covering her ears.

Love,

L

Dear Harriet,

Things continued to tick over in Khartoum. A couple came from the UK to help in our office. I don't know what we would have done without them! He was an administrator, kept the cashbox and brought order to the paper flow in the office. He trained our Sudanese Deputy Director, Richard, to work more efficiently. His wife was a primary school teacher, but she welcomed returning colleagues, making sure they found clean homes, made beds, and food upon arrival. She assisted with preparing alphabet books in various languages and offered encouragement and hospitality to whomever she met. She even gave English conversation practice to Sudanese friends.

Our work comprises more than linguistics, literacy, and translation. As these opportunities grow, we need administrators, teachers, accountants, and computer geeks. There are many opportunities for those with technical know-how to give their time and effort to fill in the gaps.

A Sudanese-American visited her family in Khartoum after an absence of three and a half years. Her mother was in failing health at eighty-five. During the first month, she was in culture shock. She didn't believe things could get worse than they had been when she and her American husband left Sudan. The exchange rate had been £s12/$1.00, but upon her return was £s450/$1.00. "The salary of a Senior Doctor was about $40 a month, and for a Junior

Doctor, it was about $20. Educated young people feel they have no future. Older middle class people are barely managing to meet the basic needs of their families. The poor are dying of disease and starvation. Malaria is rampant and many are dying of resistant malaria. Sudan is not the friendly place that formerly gathered the nations under its wings. The philosophy is for everyone to conform to the one image that the Government wants for the country. Except for a few powerful minorities, the people are not happy with this system." (Personal communication.)

After my surgery, I headed back to Kenya and Sudan in July. My abrupt departure left many tasks undone. In Kenya, I wanted to catch up with the teams and understand their needs. Our teams found Uganda more welcoming to Sudanese than Kenya. The administration was setting up a center in Entebbe where teams could work.

After being in chilly Nairobi, I asked Pam if it was hot in Khartoum. She assured me I had no fear of being cold once I arrived. "Enjoy being cold while you can."

In Khartoum, I wanted to complete the English to Cøllø Self-Instruction Transition book that defines the spelling system we have developed over the past six years. We still have a few ticklish problems to sort out, like whether to write tone. I also wanted to finish a grammar paper that Cathy and I have been working on for two years. We needed to complete it. As the Linguistic Coordinator, I wanted to be available to language teams to help them with various plans, problems, etc. Finally, we had to turn the Cøllø work over to the Cøllø Language Oversight Committee and the staff we had trained for six years.

My residence papers expire in November, so I need to renew them before returning to the US in mid-September.

Love,

L

Dear Harriet,

By July 1995, it was getting difficult to get a residence visa. Our political connections in the south lost influence during the transition to the new government. Our agreement with the southern government continued, but few of the governors will support our visas. The Sudanese man who had helped us the most needs to leave the country. His life has been threatened. Once we are gone, his life won't be worth much. So, we needed to look elsewhere to continue working in Sudan. My PhD in linguistics fit well with the needs at the University of Khartoum, and particularly at the Institute of African and Asian Studies (IAAS). John considered applying there as well, so we went for an interview.

While I had earned a doctorate, I had never applied to work as a lecturer in a university. I felt insecure and became more nervous when I saw the syllabus. We met Dr. Mahasan, the Dean of the IAAS to apply for jobs to start in January 1996. The institute is a graduate program taught in English, and they also needed help in the English and Linguistic Departments of the Faculty of Arts. Who knows where this will lead?

The university staff welcomed us with open arms. Dr. Abumanga had been teaching all the classes in the African Studies Department and was desperate for someone to join him. We said that a local salary (about $40 per month) was enough, instead of the extra dollars most foreigners expected. Sudanese instructors teach at several universities to make ends meet. So, there is a precedent for having "other things to do." I explained I had funded research, but needed a visa to be in Sudan. My application moved from the Institute to the Vice-Chancellor's office for approval to be appointed to the University.

Just after John and I left our interview, President Omar al Bashir was due to speak. We heard the Islamic students confronted him to say he was a failure because over one-hundred churches had started in Khartoum alone since he took power. That number is more than in the two previous regimes. They said if he couldn't control this trend, he was not doing a good job. There were also demonstrations by liberal students who got tear-gassed for their efforts. We were glad to have left by the time that happened.

Love,

L

Dear Harriet,

With Janice leaving to study in England for a year, we spent days clearing up piles of things around the house. The worst place was the office. No one throws anything away except me, and I'm not good at it. The piles get so DIRTY! The Cølløs continued to use the office outside the house and Acol cooked and cleaned. Any visitors who arrived stayed at the house since neither of us was there.

During my time at home, September through December, I wanted to have surgery on my eyes to correct my nearsightedness. I wore hard contact lenses in Khartoum, and with the dust, it was NOT a pleasant experience. So, when a doctor in Dallas offered to do radial keratotomy surgery for free, I took advantage of it. Mom traveled with me and found various jobs to do at the SIL center. I began preparing for my role as a linguistics professor.

As the months passed, I asked God what was going to happen. The answer I received was, *Prepare and be ready. When the time comes, you will need to leave quickly.* I purchased items to take back, upgraded my wardrobe, and enjoyed the time with Mom.

There was no guarantee. It seemed strange not to have a visa to return to Sudan. As we were working with thirty-five languages in Khartoum, my call to return remained as strong as ever.

Love,

L

Glossary of Foreign Words

Arabic

akyaas—bags

allah hu akbar—God is great

angareeb—a bed with a wooden or metal frame with rope or string for the webbing

banbur—footstool

dukhaan—smoke

Eid al-Adha—the feast of sacrifice

Eid al-Fitr—the breakfast feast

fakii—one who uses magic and charms

falafel—fried balls of chickpea paste

fatuur—breakfast

fuul—beans, particularly Egyptian beans

garmasiis—a special cloth used at weddings

guffa—basket

haboob—duststorm

hajj—the pilgrimage to Mecca

jebana—clay pot for making coffee

jebel—hill

kabba—the black stone in Mecca

kerkedeh—a drink made from hibiscus

khawajaat—foreigners

kiis—bag

kisra—crepe-like bread made from wheat and sorghum

la illah illa allah—*There is no God but Allah'*

leemun—*lime*

maa shaghaal—*not working*

ma'aleesh—sorry, too bad

medaan—open patch of land, a square

muezzin—one who is responsible for making the call to prayer five times a day

ratul—a pint measure

rotaan—gibberish, usually the word referring to local non-Arabic languages

shahari—similar to sweet shredded wheat

sheik—mayor or council leader

sinia—tray for food or roundabout

suuq—market

tobe—a long cotton or polyester cloth women use to cover their clothes and head when in public

zabuuna—female customer

zeer—an unglazed clay pot that contains drinking water

British English

flat—apartment

full stop—period, a mark of punctuation

petrol station—gas station

French

coup d'état—overthrow a government

maison—house

Cøllø (Shilluk)

dyel dhøg—the goat of asking the parents to marry their daughter

lawø—a cloth worn by men and women, tied on one shoulder

nyang—crocodile

nyaw—cat

opaj—a cowardly man who never leaves the village to hunt

rädh—king

wöö—Our Father. A greeting only for the Shilluk king.

ywög—funeral rites performed weeks or years after the person's death

Swahili

banda—a self-contained apartment

kanga—brightly covered cloth with multiple uses

References

https://www.britannica.com/topic/Gezira-Scheme

Partee, Charles. *The Story of Don McClure: Adventure in Africa* (Grand Rapids: Ministry Resources Library, Zondervan, 1990) 27

Werner, Roland, William Anderson, Andrew Wheeler. *Day of Devastation Day of Contentment, The History of the Sudanese Church Across 2000 Years.* (Nairobi: Paulines Publications, 2000)

Westermann, Diedrich. *The Shilluk People* (Westport: Negro Universities Press, 1912) LI

About Leoma Gilley

Leoma was born and raised in Chattanooga, TN, as an only child. Her father was a gifted storyteller, and she inherited that gift and continues to develop it. She obtained her BS in speech and language pathology from the University of Tennessee and worked for several years as a speech therapist. She then studied for her MA in the same field and worked in a speech and hearing clinic in Macon, GA. In 1988, she earned a PhD in Linguistics from the University of London, School of Oriental and African Studies.

Linguistics fascinated Leoma, and in 1979 she felt called to join Wycliffe Bible Translators and SIL International. This affiliation led her to more adventure than she had expected and she lived most of her adult life in Africa, about twenty years of that in the Sudan. She has traveled widely and enjoyed discovering the languages and cultures of the places she visited. After thirty-seven years, she retired and settled in Knoxville, TN.

For more great books from Peak Press
Visit Books.GracePointPublishing.com

If you enjoyed reading *Life in a Tumble Dryer*, and purchased it through an online retailer, please return to the site and write a review to help others find the book.